Appropriate Use Policies for Computers in College/University Libraries
CLIP Note #31

Compiled by

Jane Tuten
University of South Carolina Aiken
Aiken, South Carolina

Karen Junker
St. John Fisher College
Rochester, New York

College Library Information Packet Committee
College Libraries Section
Association of College and Research Libraries
A Division of the American Library Association
Chicago 2002

The paper used in this publication meets the minimum requirements of
American National Standard for Information Sciences–Permanence of
Paper for Printed Library Materials, ANSI Z39.48-1992. ∞

Library of Congress Cataloging-in-Publication Data
Appropriate use policies for computers in college/university libraries / compiled by Jane
Tuten, Karen Junker.
    p. cm. -- (CLIP note ; #31)
  Includes bibliographical references.
  ISBN 0-8389-8181-X (alk. paper)
   1. Internet access for library users--United States--Case studies. 2. Public access
computers in libraries--United States--Case studies. 3. Universities and
colleges--Computer networks--United States--Case studies. 4. Library surveys--United
States. I. Tuten, Jane H. II. Junker, Karen. III. Association of College and Research
Libraries. College Library Information Packet Committee. IV. CLIP notes ; #31.

Z692.C65 A67 2002
025.5'0285--dc21

                                    2001056746

Printed on recycled paper.

Printed in the United States of America.

06 05 04 03 02   5 4 3 2 1

TABLE OF CONTENTS

INTRODUCTION

Purpose

The purpose of this *CLIP Note* on Appropriate Use Policies for Computers in College/University Libraries is to help libraries identify desirable elements found in computer use policies and to provide guidelines for college and small university libraries that want to develop policies or have been directed to implement policies for computer usage in their library. Having a policy in place may or may not achieve the desired effect of directing appropriate use of computers. Policy implementation is an option that a library might choose to explore with the help and guidance of this *CLIP Note*.

Background

In January 2001 the *CLIP Notes* survey was sent to 266 academic libraries that serve academic institutions with enrollments between 750 and 7000 students. The institutions surveyed have been designated as Baccalaureate I or II, or Master's I or II level institutions in *The 1994 Carnegie Classification of Higher Education* (Carnegie Foundation for the Advancement of Teaching 1994). For the first time, the survey was alternatively offered electronically so that those institutions wishing to respond by electronic means could go to a website maintained by the American Library Association/Association for College and Research Libraries.

A search of the literature on acceptable use policies in academic libraries yielded a fairly high volume of articles in the late eighties, when public-use computers began appearing on a large scale. At that time, all kinds of libraries were facing issues primarily dealing with security and access, largely unaware of coming ethical and legal concerns associated with the World Wide Web and the transmission of electronic information.

During the nineties, less was written specifically about Appropriate Use Policies (AUPs) in academic libraries, probably because institutional AUPs, which were beginning to appear, covered campus libraries quite well. In 1996, the Association for Research Libraries published Information Technology Policies: a SPEC Kit. This publication provided recognition of the important role that libraries would play in the information technology revolution that was sweeping society and academia.

As the size and popularity of the World Wide Web grew, public and school libraries increasingly turned their attention to concerns about limiting access to objectionable content on the WWW through the use of filtering. Filtering is generally not an issue in higher education because of the academic commitment to intellectual freedom. In fact, the Association of College and Research Libraries has developed principles protecting this freedom, which can be found on their website (ACRL 1999).

In spite of the relative paucity of literature specifically focused on AUPs in academic libraries, there is much to be learned from general articles (Smith 1998; ALA 2000; Nicefaro 1998) on the topic. Nicefaro specifically addresses issues of employee utilization of the Internet and email, but many of the issues she addresses extend to the realm of responsible use of the Internet by the public. Academic use policies are mentioned briefly in terms of security and confidentiality.

Reilly stresses the need for a statement of purpose and examples of good practice in the school library sector. A similar model may be applied to libraries in institutions of higher education. Additionally, Reilly presents a clear explanation of the elements of an Acceptable Use Policy.

All libraries must address a common core of issues surrounding patron use of hardware, software, and electronic content. Complementing the sample policies, which are an integral part of this CLIP Note, the bibliography includes sources that contain or lead to other academic AUPs (Ebbinghouse 1997; McCollum 1999; Smith 1998; Educause 2001).

The selected bibliography contains citations and brief abstracts to sources found in journals, books, and websites published since 1996 to provide the most current and, therefore, most useful information for academic policy-makers.

Analysis

A total of 135 libraries responded to the survey, a response rate of 50.75%. Over one-third (53) of the responding libraries submitted their answers to the questionnaire electronically. Many respondents sent copies of policies or library/institutional URLs. The number of responses indicated a high level of interest in the topic among small to medium-sized academic libraries. The response rate underscored the critical need for policies to address problems and/or questions that arise as a result of the increased awareness and use of information technology in academic libraries.

Questions 1-3   Library and Institutional Characteristics

Questions 1 through 3 on the questionnaire describe the institution and the library servicing the institution. A majority (55%, 72) of libraries responding to the survey are associated with schools having enrollments that fall between 1,001 and 2,500 FTE students. FTE faculty size was in the range of 51-150 in 53% of the institutions. Ninety-eight percent or 130 of the libraries responding had 1-15 librarians employed. Eighty-six percent or 114 libraries employ between 1 and 10 librarians.

Questions 4-6   Computing Facilities

Public access computers, labs, and staffing of labs within the libraries were the subjects of questions 4 through 6. Twenty-six percent or 33 of the responding libraries stated that the institutional library provided more than 50 public-use computers, while 58% or 74 had between 11 and 40 computers. While 65% or 88 respondents had a computer lab housed in the library, technical support for the labs was provided by non-library staff in 62% (56) of the facilities. Library staff provided support in only 34 (38%) of the library computing labs. Given that a high number of libraries offer multiple computers to their users or have access to a lab on-site, it should be noted that the library staff does not routinely provide technical support.

Questions 7-9   Filtering Software, Electronic Resources and Services

Filtering software was absent in 95% (126) of the 133 responding libraries. Because of the commitment of academic libraries to the fundamental concept of intellectual freedom as stated by the American Library Association, the reported results are to be expected. The basic tenet for academic libraries ensures that the foundation for providing open access to information remains as unencumbered as possible, while affording protection for institutional technology infrastructure. A total of 108 libraries or 81% have security software installed that inhibits the ability of the patron to reconfigure the machine.

Given the rate at which libraries have embraced information technology, it came as no surprise that the impact of the technology within the reporting libraries facilitated use of a broad range of resources. Over 90% of the respondents provided basic electronic resources and services such as online catalogs (99%, 134), full-text periodical databases/titles (98%, 133), reference works (92%, 124), indexes (95%, 128), and Internet access (99%, 134). Course reserve lists (64%, 86), electronically accessed files and aids created by library faculty/staff (53%, 71), reference service by email (64%, 87), ILL requests (77%, 104), acquisitions requests (54%, 73) and other more individualized services were reported by over 50% of libraries. Computers not dedicated to library functions (60%, 81), scanners (45%, 61), and non-library software applications (68%, 92) were reported as available for patron use in many instances.

Many libraries offer services that support other programs on their campuses that may be delivered through alternative methods such as distance education (38%, 51), video/desktop conferencing (13%, 17), and satellite broadcasting or down-linking (24%, 32). Numerous libraries provide assistive technology to aid patrons with disabilities through the provision of special stations and software (39%, 53).

Additional electronic resources and services that were reported as available for patrons were streaming audio for music reserves, media equipment booking, mapping software, a digital microfilm reader, a poster maker, and wireless computing facilities.

Question 10   Libraries/IT Departments

When the enormous impact of the information technology revolution became apparent to forward-looking institutions in the early 1980s, some combined computer departments and libraries, the primary and logical users of the technology. However, among the respondents to this survey, most libraries (91%, 123) reported that they were separate from the information technology or computing departments of their institutions. Many respondents urged a strong working relationship between the units, even if they were not administratively combined.

Library Policies

Questions 11-23   Policy Development, Issues, Consequences

Approximately half (69) of the respondents to the survey had their own library appropriate-use policy. The majority of the policies (87%) had been developed since 1995. More than 34% had been developed or revised since 1999. Policies were developed for a variety of reasons, with over 70% citing such justifications as the need to address existing problems (77%, 53), to address potential problems (83%, 57), and the conviction that policies were generally a good idea (71%, 49). A few of the responding libraries stated that the state (3%, 2) or the institution (1%, 1) mandated the policies. One library reported the necessity to develop a policy to receive grant funds. The majority (52%, 35) of libraries revise their policies at least every two years with 62% of the policies revisited in 2000 or 2001.

Library mission statements were considered by 84% (59) of the libraries with appropriate-use policies, while 11% (8) of the respondents did not know if the library mission statement had been considered. Librarians and the library director worked together with support staff to develop most policies (89%, 58). Websites (52%, 34) and other libraries (85%, 56) provided the major sources of information about policies, followed by journal articles (38%, 25) and other institutions (39%, 26). Key issues addressed are:
- Internet access (74%, 51),
- monopolization of equipment (64%, 44),
- email misuse (61%, 42),
- patron identity (55%, 38),
- deliberate mischief (45%, 31),
- harassment (41%, 28),
- copyright (39%, 27),

- abuse of hardware (35%, 24),
- excessive printing (33%, 23),
- consequences of both major/minor violations (32%, 22),
- hacking (26%, 18),
- commercial use (26%, 18),
- network overload (6%, 4),
- sharing of personal password (10%, 7),
- enforcement mechanisms (16%, 11).

Additional issues were addressed in 25% (17) of the policies according to the responses to the questionnaire. Items covered included civility, obscenity or pornography, license abuse, time limits for visitors, children under 16, downloading, intellectual property rights, games and recreational chat room use, and plagiarism. Librarians (100%, 69) and library support staff (71%, 49) were the principle enforcers of the policies. Campus security was reported as providing support by 39% (27) of the respondents. The majority of respondents (67%, 46) reported that they rarely used or cited the policy to enforce a violation. While responding libraries typically have policies in place, policies are not used for enforcement purposes. Policies provide clarification and define appropriate use of computers for support staff and librarians, thereby providing a strong framework for limits and parameters of use. Individual judgment would then come into play.

Consequences surrounding violations were varied. Principle consequences included asking violators to stop (67%, 46), calling campus security (46%, 32), reporting the incident to the Library Director (46%, 32), and revocation of library privileges (30%, 21). A total of 25% (17) of the respondents reported the violators to the Dean of Students and 16% (11) were reported to the Information Technology Director or someone in a similar role. Only one library imposed a monetary fine. Other consequences reported included calling the local police, asking the violator to leave, and barring the violator from the library if not a college student. Slightly more than half (54%, 37) stated that no documentation is kept concerning the violations and any actions taken. Forty-six percent (32) reported keeping documentation of the violations.

Question 24   Posting of Policies

Most libraries reported that the policies were posted near the public access computer terminals (77%, 53). Others posted them on the library website or homepage (42%, 29). Fifteen (22%) reported that the policies were included in the library manual. Three (4%) libraries used the policy as a screen saver or wallpaper for public access library computers. Three (4%) libraries reported that the policy was not printed or posted.

Questions 25-26   Effects

The majority (81%, 56) of the responding libraries reported that there had been no complaints regarding any part of the policy. A total of 13 (19%) of the respondents reported some complaints. Complaints were related to use by off-campus users, use of email, hours of the labs, need for instruction after hours, and time limits when no one is waiting.

An overwhelming majority (93%, 64) of the respondents reported that the policies had the desired effect.

Institutional Policies

Questions 27-34   Policy Development

Campus-wide institutional policies are more prevalent than library policies among the respondents to the questionnaire. A total of 85% (109) of the respondents have institutional policies, compared to 51% (69) library-specific policies. The majority (61%, 55) of the institutional policies were developed between 1995 and 1998. Generally, these policies existed earlier than the majority of the library policies. Only 17% (15) were developed between 1999 and 2001.

The majority of responding libraries offered the same reasons for institutional policies as they did for library policies. The top three reasons were the same. A total of 84% (85) were addressing potential problems, 72% (73) believed that policies were generally a good idea, and for 71% (72) institutional policies were written to address existing problems. Additional responses noted that 22% (22) were mandated by the institution's administration and 2% (2) were mandated by state law. Other reasons for policy development included requirements by Internet Service Providers, network overload issues, mandate by committee, and software copyright licenses. While many policies are updated at least every two years (41%, 41), many respondents were not aware of the frequency of revision. A total of 60% (51) libraries reported a revision of institutional policy in 2000 or 2001, while 13% (13) never revise.

Institutional mission statements were considered by 55% (58) of the respondents during the development of the institutional policies with 14% (15) stating that they were not. Almost one-third (31%, 32) of the responding libraries stated that they did not know if the institutional mission statement had been considered during policy development. Development of an institutional policy generally involved the Head of Information Technology (64%, 66) and the administration (42%, 43). Over one-third (34%, 35) had the involvement of a campus-wide committee during policy development. Other institutions (77%, 72), websites (54%, 50), conferences and workshops (34%, 32), and journal articles (30%, 28) provided major sources of information during policy development.

Question 35   Issues

Concerns addressed most frequently by institutional policies were user/patron identity (87%, 94) and email misuse (83%, 90). Copyright, Internet access, hacking, and deliberate mischief were addressed by 81% of the institutional policies. Eighty-eight policies addressed copyright and hacking while Internet access and deliberate mischief were addressed by 87 of the institutional policies. Harassment was addressed by 80% (86) of the institutions. Other issues concerning appropriate use of computers addressed by institutional policies were commercial use (74%, 80), sharing of personal password (72%, 78), abuse of hardware (57%, 62), network overload (56%, 61), and monopolizing of equipment (38%, 41). Enforcement mechanisms were addressed in 52% (56) of the policies while 47% (51) dealt with consequences of policy violation.

Questions 36-39   Enforcement and Consequences

Administrative staff (78%, 82) and campus security (24%, 25) enforce institutional policies most often. Policies are rarely used or cited to enforce a violation (31%, 33), although 56% (59) reported that the respondents did not know if they were used in enforcement. The most common consequences of violations of the institutional policy are: asked to stop (79%, 84), reported to the Dean of Students (64%, 68), reported to the IT Director (58%, 61), and lab privileges revoked (57%, 60). A total of 78.12% (75) document violations and/or actions taken, 10% do not, and 11% (11) do not know if the library documents offenses.

Questions 40-41   Posting of Policies

The most common means of publicizing the policy is posting on the campus website (80%, 85), followed by printing the policy in the student handbook (58%, 61) and posting near computers (29%, 31). A total of 49% (50) of the respondents said that the policy had the desired effect, while 48% (48) responded that they did not know. Only 3% (3) of respondents thought that the policy had not had the desired effect.

No Policies

Question 42   Libraries and Universities Without Policies

A total of 45 of the respondents answered the question that asked why there was not a library policy or an institutional policy. Of the 45 respondents, 22% (10) stated that there was a library policy in progress while 18% (8) reported that there was an institutional policy in progress. Only 16% (7) stated that a policy was not needed.

Advice Offered

Many of the responding libraries reflected and shared thoughts or advice on the process of developing and implementing a policy on the appropriate use of computers. Many stressed clear, general, flexible policies that were uniform across campus. Others stated that consistent enforcement was the key to a successful policy, and that drafts should be widely circulated with broad campus involvement of the academic community, including students, faculty, and staff.

One respondent stressed the need to communicate library-specific issues, thereby avoiding questions of access or statements contrary to the library's support of privacy. Others stressed the need for review by legal counsel to ensure conformity to state and local law. One respondent suggested that neither library nor computer staff should be put into the role of enforcer and that since misuse was a behavioral issue, channels that were already in place, such as campus security, should handle offenders.

Respondents writing suggestions for those considering library policies stressed the need to consult appropriate use policies that had been developed by others. Review at the highest administrative level on campus was also a frequent suggestion, as was the need to post the policy within clear view of public access computers. Several used the policy in quite innovative ways, in that policies were utilized as wallpaper or screen savers on public terminals.

Conclusion

Most libraries and institutions consider Appropriate Use Policies important and critical documents needed by librarians and other academicians, so that they may address existing and potential problems associated with the rapid increase in use and development of new technologies. As stated by McCollum, "In Internet time, new ways to misbehave online come faster than institutions can create policies to deal with them" (p. A35).

As rapid changes occur in the global community, both libraries and institutions of higher education must meet their responsibility to prepare students to effectively integrate into the workforce and society. At the same time, students must be taught the appropriate and ethical use of computers. Policies outline both rights and responsibilities, complete with the consequences of misuse.

At least 85% of responding libraries looked to other libraries for ideas or models in the design and content of their policies. This *CLIPNote* will facilitate the sharing process as libraries create and update their policies by offering both text examples and individual URLs to encourage further investigation. An auxiliary benefit of this publication is the ability to compare one's own facilities, services, and equipment to those in similar sized libraries.

This *CLIPNote* on Appropriate Use Policies and the accompanying list of URLs will provide a discussion of the pros and cons along with examples of current policies, thereby enabling libraries to develop and adapt policies that best suit their needs and institutions.

SELECTED BIBLIOGRAPHY

SELECTED BIBLIOGRAPHY

ACRL. Intellectual Freedom Principles for Academic Libraries. www.ala.org/acrl/principles.html (2000).

ALA. Guidelines for the Development of Policies and Procedures Regarding User Behavior and Library Usage. www.ala.org/alaorg/oif/usage.html (2000).

Cordell, Rosanne M. and Nancy A. Wootton. "Institutional Policy Issues for Providing
Public Internet Access." Reference Services Review 24, no. 1 (1996): 7-12, 56.

Examination of issues to consider when developing Internet access policies for all types of libraries.

Ebbinghouse, Carol and Robert Giblin. "Taming the Wicked, Wicked Net: Acceptable
Use and the Internet." Searcher 5, no. 7 (Jul-Aug 1997): 12, 14, 16-23, 25.

Full discussion of ways to prevent improper usage of online access in a variety of environments. Includes related article detailing the development and content of Western State University College of Law's draft acceptable use policy. Useful bibliographies.

Educause - Items with an index of Acceptable Use/Ethics Policies. www.educause.edu/asp/doclib/subject_docs.asp?Term_ID=110 (2001).

Impressive listing of links to academic institutions' AUP's.

Hyman, Karen. "Internet Policies: Managing in the Real World." American Libraries
28, no. 10 (Nov 1997): 60-62.

Reality, solutions, and pitfalls of Internet policies. No perfect solution.

Jones, Barbara M. Libraries, Access and Intellectual Freedom: Developing Policies for Public and Academic Libraries. Chicago: American Library Association, 1999.

" . . . written to help academic and public librarians make their professional ideals a reality through policies that promote access to information for user communities." Intellectual freedom point-of-view. Policy development is focus of the book. Includes guide-lines from ALA's Intellectual Freedom Committee for publicly funded libraries, pp. 174-176.

Leung, Shirley and Diane Bisom. <u>Information Technology Policies: a SPEC Kit.</u> Washington,
        D.C.: Association for Research Libraries, Office of Management Services, 1996.

        While only 39 ARL institutions are sampled, the SPEC Kit documents policies governing the use of computing resources and electronic infor-mation crafted in the mid-1990's. The kit's institutional and library documents contain such items as email policies, WWW policies, computer acquisition policies, and employee or public computer use policies.

McCollum, Kelly. "On Line, Ways to Misbehave Can Outpace College Rules." <u>The Chronicle of Higher Education</u> 46, no. 4 (Sep 17, 1999): A35-A36.

        Provides discussion and examples of AUP's from Salisbury State, University of Oregon, Harvey Mudd College, Indiana University, University of Georgia, Clayton College and State University. Includes a list of sample academic computer use policies on the web.

Nicefaro, Melissa Everett. "Internet Use Policies." <u>Online</u> 22, no. 5 (Sept/Oct 1998): 31-33.

        Discusses Internet and computer use policies in corporate, public, and academic library settings detailing elements to include.

Reilly, Rob. "Laying Down the Law: Crafting Acceptable Use Policy." <u>Multimedia Schools</u>
        7, no. 5 (Oct 2000): 78-80.

        Although geared to elementary/secondary school environments, article presents basic concepts applicable in other arenas. Provides URL's for school AUP's for examination of good and bad points.

Smith, Mark. <u>Internet Policy Handbook for Libraries</u>. New York: Neal-Schuman Publishers, Inc., 1998.

        Systematically examines elements of an Internet policy. Explores potential positive and negative impacts. Extracts and full-content of actual policies, most with URL's. ". . . organizes and analyzes the range of policies that libraries are using to manage Internet access." [p. vi]. Appendix includes complete policies from University of Pennsylvania and Holy Cross University. Also an Internet Policy Checklist.

CLIP Note **SURVEY RESULTS**

QUESTIONNAIRE
ON
APPROPRIATE USE POLICIES FOR COMPUTERS
IN
COLLEGE/UNIVERSITY LIBRARIES

Institutions: Public 35   Private 100

ALL FIGURES REQUESTED SHOULD BE FOR FALL 1999 OR FOR FISCAL YEAR 1999-2000. THE FOLLOWING STATISTICS REQUESTED ARE BASED ON IPEDS SURVEY CATEGORIES AND DEFINITIONS.

---

1. Number of full-time equivalent (FTE) students

   130 responses

   Average: 2546.11   range: 593 - 7748   median: 2216

2. Number of full-time equivalent (FTE) faculty

   122 responses

   Average: 156.67   range: 32 – 394   median: 138

3. Number of full-time equivalent (FTE) librarians

   133 responses

   Average: 6.81   range: 2 – 19   median: 6

4. How many public use computers, including lab computers, are located in the library?

   128 responses

   Average: 41.10   range: 4 – 180   median: 31

5. Is there a computer lab within the library?

   135 responses

88 (65%) Yes   47 (35%) No

6. If there is a lab, is it staffed by the library?

90 responses

34 (38%) Yes   56 (62%) No

7. Does the Library have filtering software installed on public workstations?

133 responses

 7 (5%) Yes   126 (95%) No

8. Does the Library have software installed on public workstations that controls the ability of the patron to reconfigure the machine?

133 responses

108 (81%) Yes   25 (19%) No

9. Please check any of the **electronic resources and services** that are available to patrons for use in your Library:

135 Responses

134 (99%) Catalog
134 (99%) Internet access
133 (98%) Full-text periodicals
128 (95%) Indexes
124 (92%) Reference titles
104 (77%) ILL requests
 92 (68%) Computer software for patron use (e.g. word-processing, spreadsheet, etc.)
 87 (64%) Reference service by email
 86 (64%) Course reserve list
 81 (60%) Computers not dedicated to library functions
 73 (54%) Acquisitions requests
 71 (53%) Files and aids created by library faculty/staff
 61 (45%) Scanning equipment
 53 (39%) Technology to assist patrons with disabilities (e.g. specially equipped stations)
 51 (38%) Support for Distance Education classes
 49 (36%) Library instruction request
 44 (33%) Library tutorial
 41 (30%) Full-text course reserves

32 (24%) Satellite broadcasting or down-linking
17 (13%) Video/desktop conferencing
15 (11%) Other (please explain)

10. Is the Library separate from the Information Technology/Computer Services department?

135 responses

123 (91%) Yes   12 (9%) No

11. Does the Library have its own policy on computer use?

134 responses

69 (51%) Yes   65 (48%) No

PLEASE ENCLOSE SAMPLES OF YOUR LIBRARY/INSTITUTIONAL POLICIES, URLs, OR ANY OTHER DOCUMENTATION RELATED TO COMPUTER USE THAT YOU BELIEVE WOULD BE HELPFUL.

If yes to question 11, please continue. If no to question 11, skip to question 27.

12. What year was the policy developed?

69 responses

1	(1%)	1987	7	(10%)	1995	10	(15%)	1999
2	(3%)	1989	8	(12%)	1996	12	(18%)	2000
1	(1%)	1993	6	(9%)	1997	1	(1%)	2001
3	(4%)	1994	15	(22%)	1998	1	(1%)	Ongoing
						2	(3%)	Don't know

13. Why was the policy developed? Check all that apply.

69 Responses

57 (83%) Address potential problems
53 (77%) Address existing problems
49 (71%) Generally a good idea
 5 (7%) Other (please explain)
 2 (3%) Mandated by State

1 (1%) Mandated by the administration

14. Was the Library's mission statement considered during the development of the policy?

70 Responses

59 (84%) Yes   8 (11%) No   2 (3%) Don't know
 1 (1%) Do not have mission statement

15. How often is the policy revised or revisited?

67 Responses

24 (36%) Every year
11 (16%) Every two years
 9 (13%) Every five years
 3 (5%) Never
20 (30%) Other (please explain)

16. In what year was the policy last revised?

55 responses

1 (2%) 1995	9 (16%) 1999	1 (2%) Don't know
4 (7%) 1997	29 (53%) 2000	1 (2%) Not in yet
4 (7%) 1998	5 (9%) 2001	1 (2%) In process

17. Who developed the Library policy? Check all that apply.

65 Responses

33 (51%) Librarians
33 (51%) Library Director
25 (38%) Librarians and library support staff
 8 (12%) Head of Information Technology
 7 (11%) Campus Library committee
 4 (6%) Other campus-wide group
 2 (3%) Other (please explain)

18. What outside sources were consulted during the development of the policy? Check all that apply.

66 Responses

56 (85%) Other libraries
34 (52%) Web sites
26 (39%) Other institutions
25 (38%) Journal articles
17 (26%) Listservs
 8 (12%) Other (please explain)
 5 (8%) Books
 4 (6%) ARL SPEC Kit 218

19. What issues/topics are addressed in the policy? Check all that apply.

69 Responses

51 (74%) Internet access
44 (64%) Monopolizing equipment
42 (61%) E-mail misuse
38 (55%) User/patron identity (student, faculty, staff, community)
31 (45%) Deliberate mischief
28 (41%) Harassment
27 (39%) Copyright
24 (35%) Abuse of hardware
23 (33%) Excessive printing
22 (32%) Consequences of violations (minor and major)
18 (26%) Commercial use
18 (26%) Hacking
17 (25%) Other (please explain)
11 (16%) Enforcement mechanisms
 7 (10%) Sharing of personal password
 4 (6%) Network overload

20. Who enforces the policy in the library? Check all that apply.

69 Responses

69 (100%) Librarian
49 (71%) Support staff
27 (39%) Campus security
 4 (6%) Other (please explain)

21. How frequently is the policy used/cited to enforce a violation? Check one.

69 Responses

46 (67%) Rarely

14 (20%) Weekly
 6 (9%) Monthly
 2 (3%) At least once a day
 1 (1 %) Never

22. What are the consequences of a violation of the policy? Check all that apply.

69 Responses

46 (67%) Asked to stop
32 (46%) Campus security called
32 (46%) Reported to Library Director
21 (30%) Library privileges revoked
17 (25%) Reported to Dean of Students
11 (16%) Reported to IT Director
 8 (12%) Other (please explain)
 1 (1%) Monetary fine imposed

23. Are violations of the policy and any actions taken documented?

69 Responses

32 (46%) Yes   37 (54%) No

24. How is the policy publicized to library patrons? Check all that apply.

69 Responses

53 (77%) Posted near computers
29 (42%) Library website/homepage
15 (22%) Printed in library manual
 3 (4%) Not posted or publicized
 0 (0%) Printed in campus bulletin

25. Have there been complaints concerning any part of the policy? If there have been complaints, what parts have been referenced?

69 responses

13 (19%) Yes   56 (81%) No

26. Has the policy had the desired effect?

69 responses

64 (93%) Yes   2 (3%) No   3 (4%) Other

27. Is there an Institution-wide policy on computer use?

128 responses

109 (85%) Yes   19 (15%) No

PLEASE ENCLOSE SAMPLES OF YOUR LIBRARY/INSTITUTIONAL POLICIES, URLs, OR ANY OTHER DOCUMENTATION RELATED TO COMPUTER USE THAT YOU BELIEVE WOULD BE HELPFUL.

If yes to question 27, please continue. If no to question 27, skip to question 42.

28. What year was the policy developed?

100 responses

1 (1%) 1983	1 (1%) 1990	14 (14%) 1995	6 (6%) 2000
2 (2%) 1984	1 (1%) 1991	15 (15%) 1996	1 (1%) 2001
2 (2%) 1985	1 (1%) 1992	12 (12%) 1997	14 (14%) Don't Know
1 (1%) 1987	3 (3%) 1993	14 (14%) 1998	
1 (1%) 1989	4 (4%) 1994	8 (8%) 1999	

29. Why was the policy developed? Check all that apply.

101 Responses

85 (84%) Address potential problems
73 (72%) Generally a good idea
72 (71%) Address existing problems
22 (22%) Mandated by the administration
 7 (7%) Other (please explain)
 2 (2%) Mandated by State law

30. Was the Institutional mission statement considered during the development of the policy?

105 Responses

58 (55%) Yes   15 (14%) No   32 (31%) Don't know
 0 (0%) Do not have mission statement

31. How often is the policy revised or revisited? Check one.

100 Responses

42 (42%) Other (please explain
29 (29%) Every year
13 (13%) Never
12 (12%) Every two years
 4 (4%) Every five years

32. In what year was the policy last revised?

85 Responses

2 (2%)   1994   5 (6%) 1998   1 (1%) Never
1 (1%) 1995   9 (11%)   1999   9 (11%)   Not Sure/Don't know
1 (1%) 1996   47 (55%) 2000
6 (7%) 1997   4 (5%) 2001

33. Who developed the institutional policy? Check all that apply.

103 Responses

66 (64%) Head of Information Technology
43 (42%) Administration
35 (34%) Campus-wide committee
24 (23%) Faculty
19 (18%) Other (please explain)

34. What outside sources were consulted during the development of the policy? Check all that apply.

93 Responses

72 (77%) Other institutions
50 (54%) Web sites
32 (34%) Conferences and workshops
28 (30%) Journal articles
20 (22%) Listservs
20 (22%) Other (please explain)
11 (12%) Books

35. What issues/topics are addressed in the policy? Check all that apply.

108 Responses

94 (87%) User/patron identity
90 (83%) E-mail misuse
88 (81%) Copyright
88 (81%) Hacking
87 (81%) Internet access
87 (81%) Deliberate mischief
86 (80%) Harassment
80 (74%) Commercial use
78 (72%) Sharing of personal password
62 (57%) Abuse of hardware
61 (56%) Network overload
56 (52%) Enforcement mechanisms
51 (47%) Consequences of violations (minor and major)
41 (38%) Monopolizing equipment
32 (30%) Excessive printing
 8 (7%) Other (please explain)

36. Who enforces the policy? Check all that apply.

105 Responses

82 (78%) Administrative staff
27 (26%) Other (please explain)
25 (24%) Campus security
17 (16%) Faculty

37. How frequently is the policy used/cited to enforce a violation? Check one

105 responses

59 (56%) Don't Know
33 (31%) Rarely
10 (10%) Monthly
 2 (2%) At least once a day
 1 (1%) Weekly

38. What are the consequences of a violation of the policy? Check all that apply.

106 Responses

84 (79%) Asked to stop

68 (64%) Reported to Dean of Students
61 (58%) Reported to IT Director
60 (57%) Lab privileges revoked
39 (37%) Campus security called
33 (31%) Other (please explain)
 6 (6%) Monetary fine imposed

39. Are violations of the policy and any actions taken documented?

96 Responses

75 (78.12%) Yes   10 (10.41%) No   11 (11.46%) Don't Know

40. How is the policy publicized campus-wide? Check all that apply.

106 Responses

85 (80%) Campus website/homepage
61 (58%) Printed in student handbook
31 (29%) Posted near computers
13 (12%) Printed in campus bulletin
 5 (5%) Not posted or publicized
 3 (3%) Other

41. Has the policy had the desired effect?

101 Responses

50 (49%) Yes   3 (3%) No   48 (48%) Don't know

42. Why is there **not** a Library or Institution policy? Check all that apply.

45 Responses

11 (24%) Other (please explain)
10 (22%) Policy in progress by the library
 8 (18%) Policy in progress by the institution
 7 (16%) Not needed
 6 (13%) No time to write one
 3 (7%) Don't know

43. What advice would you offer to libraries/institutions that are beginning the process of developing/implementing a policy on the appropriate use of computers?

45 Responses

PLEASE ENCLOSE SAMPLES OF YOUR LIBRARY/INSTITUTIONAL POLICIES, URLs, OR ANY OTHER DOCUMENTATION RELATED TO COMPUTER USE THAT YOU BELIEVE WOULD BE HELPFUL.

URL for applicable policies (in lieu of print policies):

_____

Please check below if sample documents can be published in a *CLIP Note* publication.

_____I give permission to publish any documents I send with this completed survey in a *CLIP Note* publication.

_____Permission to publish in a *CLIP Note* publication any document I send with this completed survey requires this copyright statement:

_____

_____

_____

Thank you for your cooperation with this survey.
For your convenience, a self-addressed envelope is enclosed. Please return the survey and any documents by January 31, 2001, to: Jane H. Tuten, USC Aiken Library, 471 Parkway, Aiken, SC 29801

APPROPRIATE USE DOCUMENTS

APPROPRIATE USE DOCUMENTS

Library AUPs

General
Info &
Services

Library
Instruction

Electronic
Information
Sources

Interlibrary
Loan

Distance Ed

ASC Home

Computer Resources

Joel J. Jensen Computer Lab

Information regarding this lab can be found here.

Research Computers

Seven computers are located straight north of the Joel J. Jensen Computer Lab on the second floor of the library. Four of these computers are for ASC student use only and function just as do the computers in the Joel J. Jensen Computer Lab. The remaining three computers are available for community use. The community computers offer Internet and various CD titles.

Marmot Terminals

The ASC library catalog is kept on a computer system named Marmot. Through Marmot terminals, patrons may access the holdings of ASC and many other libraries around the nation. Periodical and specialty databases may also be accessed. Marmot terminals are located on all three floors of the library.

Policies Concerning Computer Use by ASC Students

The ASC Nielsen Library does not place any restrictions on ASC student computer usage other than those which are in place campus-wide. This includes, but may not be restricted to: Acceptable Use Policy, Electronic Communications Policy, Web Page Policy, and Student Web Page Policy.

Policies Concerning Computer Use by Community Patrons

The primary purpose of ASC Library is to serve the college's students, faculty, and staff. Secondarily the library will serve community patrons. The more resources which are available to the library, the higher is the level of service which the library may provide. When resources are scarce, the library may need to cut back on services to the community in order to adequately service its primary users -- ASC students, faculty, and staff.

At a minimum, community patrons will be provided with some computer access to facilitate research via Internet, CDs, and other electronic resources. The following are not considered to be necessary for research and thus are not permitted: games, chatlines, or word processing.

E-mail is allowed but the library is not responsible for providing enough computers to meet the community's desire for this activity. The library only agrees to provide enough computer access to facilitate a certain level of research...similar to that provided by the library's print collection.

Because students should not be asked to fund the computer use of community patrons, computers used by the community will be provided and maintained apart from student fees. This includes printer toner and paper.

When other patrons are waiting, community patrons will be asked to restrict their computer usage to 30 minutes at any one time.

Community patrons must follow ASC's computing guidelines, including the Acceptable Use Policy and the Electronic Communications Policy.

Because ASC wishes to have a good rapport with local communities and with potential future ASC students, no age restriction is placed on community computer usage. Users of all ages may have valid research needs. However, any patron who is abusing computer hardware, disturbing other patrons, or otherwise violating policies will be asked to leave the computer area.

Contact Us
Adams State College
Alamosa, CO 81102
This site and its contents © 1999 - 2001 Adams State College

ANGELO STATE UNIVERSITY

PORTER HENDERSON LIBRARY

8 December 2000

POLICY & PROCEDURE MEMORANDUM #10 29 February 2000

INTERNET USAGE ON LIBRARY TERMINALS

Back

The acceptable use of the Library's terminals is in support of research, instructional, administrative, and other intellectual pursuits consistent with the Library's and Angelo State University's mission and objectives. Users are expected to follow all University policies related to computer resources. The Library assumes no responsibility for damages, direct or indirect, arising from the use of the Library's terminals, on-line information services, and/or equipment.

I. Primary Users.

A. Members of the Angelo State University Community (students, faculty, and staff)

are authorized to use the Library's terminals.

B. Because some information service subscriptions may require access that is

restricted to the ASU Community, a separate terminal(s) will be set aside for non-ASU community members.

C. Due to limited resources, users must not make unreasonable use of the services and equipment provided.

II. Primary Use.

A. Access to RAMCAT (on-line public access catalog) and RAMNET (gateway to Web based information services subscriptions) and other networked or locally mounted information resources.

B. Access to the Library's and University's homepages.

III. Secondary Use.

A. Searching Internet-related resources and sites.

B. University related functions such as registration, checking student records, etc.

IV. Unacceptable Use.

A. E-mail.

B. Chat room access, MUDING, game playing, or other similar activities.

C. Violation of U. S. copyright laws and licensing agreements.

D. Downloading of text files, software, executable files, databases and similar "live" technology to university disk drives.

E. Removing, relocating, modification, or destruction of University owned hardware, software, or data display and desktop configurations.

F. Downloading of computer viruses.

G. Use must not be disruptive or of a nature that other users in the vicinity find to be harassing or disruptive.

H. Attempted evasion of system and network security measures.

I. Infringement of the security or privacy of either University or non-university computer systems and/or other individuals.

V. Reservations.

A. The Library and Information Technology representatives reserve the right to regularly delete files from system and network hard drives.

B. The Library reserves the right to impose time limitations on the use of the Library's terminals.

VI. Enforcement.

A. Library staff members have the right to enforce this policy; obtain University

Police aid for assistance in the enforcement of Library and University policies and procedures, state and federal laws, and *Regent's Rules and Regulations*; and to deny access for violations of provisions. The University's disciplinary policy will govern loss of privileges.

B. Any user objecting to the provisions or enforcement of this policy of may follow

the established University appeals process.

Back

Workstation and Internet Access Policy

Library's Computer Workstations Use and Internet Access Policy

Adopted 4 May 1998
Revised 6 August 1999

The primary purpose of the ASU West Library's computer workstations is to provide access to the library's bibliographic databases and the Internet to support ASU West's students, faculty and staff with their academic research. Priority in the use of the computer workstations and other library resources will be given to ASU students, faculty and staff conducting academic research. Patrons using the workstations for Internet browsing not related to academic research or for personal communications or entertainment (e.g. Web-based e-mail, chat and games) can be asked to vacate the station when workstations are needed by those needing to conduct research.

ASU West librarians and staff offer assistance, guidance, and instruction on using the Internet as a research and information resource. We do not monitor and have no control over the information accessed on the computers within the library, in accordance with our educational mission and the principles of free speech.* We cannot be held responsible for content or resources other than those we have developed, such as the ASU West Library's Web pages.

Internet users in the library should be aware of and respect the desires of others not to be inadvertently exposed to material and images they find offensive.

Users may not use library workstations for the purpose of illegal activity or tamper with the workstations' configurations, software, hardware or operating system. Any act of hacking or illegal use of the workstations will be reported immediately to the campus police (DPS) and offenders will be prosecuted in accordance with ARS 13-2316 and 18 USCS 1030.

As with other library resources, parents or legal guardians are responsible for their children's use of the Internet in the library.

For more information about this policy, contact the library's administration offices at 543-8518.

*Note: The ASU West Library subscribes to the principles on freedom of speech in the American Library Association's Library Bill of Rights (http://www.ala.org/work/freedom/lbr.html). Copies are available at the Reference Desk.

Home	Library Catalog	Article Databases	Internet Searching	How Do I...?	Search Our Site

Last Modified: Monday February 12 2001, DI

INTERNET ACCEPTABLE USE POLICY

The Athens State University Library provides Internet access as a service to its patrons: students, faculty, and staff of the Athens State University and members of the local community.

Guidelines for acceptable use:

1. Internet use shall be limited to educational purposes. These educational purposes include research that fulfills class assignments or promotes general knowledge gathering.

2. Library computers shall not be used to play games, enter chat rooms, or other recreational activities.

3. Library computers shall not be used for sending or receiving e-mail. Students needing access to e-mail are advised to use computer labs on campus.

4. During times of high demand, patrons will be asked to limit their use of library computers to 30 minutes.

5. The Internet is a global electronic network with a highly diverse user population. The Athens State University Library does not monitor or have control over the information accessed through the Internet and cannot be held responsible for its content. Comments on the contents of any home page should be directed to the appropriate page authors. The Athens State University Library endorses the Library Bill of Rights and the Freedom to Read statement of the American Library Association. It does not censor access to material or protect users from offensive and /or inaccurate or incorrect information. However, it fully supports the University's commitment to civility as key to the meaningful exchange of ideas. Therefore, the library's public workstations are not to be used with the intent to intimidate, harass, or display hostility toward others (e.g. hate literature, pornography, etc.). Users are also asked to be sensitive to material that others in a public place might find offensive.

6. Library computers may not be used to load patron's software or download to local drives.

7. The Library provides laser printing from its computer workstations. Users are responsible for the print jobs they request. Athens State University Library does not provide refunds for unwanted print jobs.

Library Computer Use Policy

Reese Library Research computers are provided for educational research by Augusta State University students, faculty and staff. When not being used by our primary clientele for educational research, they may be otherwise utilized.

Additional guidelines:

1. ASU students, faculty and staff always have priority.

2. When others are waiting, use is restricted to a **30 minute** period.

3. Children must be directly supervised by an adult.

4. Any harassing, illegal, or in any way disruptive use of the computers will not be tolerated. Those people in violation of this policy will be asked to terminate their use of the computer immediately.

For additional information, see the Augusta State University Computer and Network Usage Policy at: http://www.aug.edu/computing_resources/acpol.html

Created 7/98
Reviewed 4/99
Reviewed 4/00

Corriher-Linn-Black Library   **December 1998**
Catawba College   **Acceptable Use Policy**

The original date for an Internet Use Policy was established on September 28, 1998. The following Acceptable Use Policy was modified and adopted on December 2, 1998.

General

Catawba College, within the scope of its operations, provides computer resources to authorized users only. It is the aim of the college to provide an academic environment that promotes and fosters access to knowledge and the sharing of information between the college and other institutions without the fear that their work will be violated by misrepresentation, tampering, destruction or theft.

The following outlines the Acceptable Use Policy adopted by the Corriher-Linn-Black Library at Catawba College.

Authorized Users

1. Faculty, staff, and enrolled students may be authorized to utilize College computer resources. Members of the general public may have authorized access to computers in the Corriher-Linn-Black Library.
2. Any student or faculty member desiring authorization to use computer resources shall make application to the Department of Computer Services. Community Borrowers over the age of 16 shall be allowed to access to the public computers in the library. This access is limited to use of the library's OPAC (online public access catalog), NC Live (North Carolina Libraries for Virtual Education) and for other research purposes.
3. Upon approval of the application, each authorized user of the system will be provided with various security measures to protect those resources. At a minimum, this will include the issuance of a distinct password for each user. Community Borrowers have a designated password and will be logged onto the computer by a library employee.
4. Users are not to share security measures (passwords). Therefore, every user assumes full responsibility for all use pursuant to his/her security measure, whether authorized or not, and recognizes that his/her assigned resources may be suspended or terminated for the improper use of resources by himself/herself or by one utilizing his/her security measure. Catawba College recommends that users change their passwords frequently.
5. Users may not attempt to gain access to another user's account or files and may not erase or modify any application, configuration, or data files not specifically the user's own.

Internet Use

1. Internet access may not be used for any commercial purpose whatsoever.
2. The receipt or transmission of materials on the Internet in violation of any U.S. law, law of the state of North Carolina, or policy of Catawba College is strictly prohibited.
3. College resources may not be used to attempt to gain access to any computer system, on or off-campus, to which the user does not have proper authorization.
4. Violation of procedure relating to the use of the Internet may subject the user to termination of access and to other disciplinary action as set forth herein.
5. Children under the age of 16 must be accompanied by an adult who will assume full responsibility for determining appropriate Internet usage.

Printing

1. Users are not to print multiple copies of any documents.
2. Users must accept any limitations on printing, such as a restricted allowance of laser-printed pages, which the College may deem necessary in order to preserve computing resources.
3. Student printing from all public access computers will have paper deducted from the allowance set by Computer Services. Currently this allotment is 250 sheets per semester additional pages may be purchased from Computer Services.
4. Community Borrowers will be charged .10 per printed page.

COMPUTER USE IN L.P. HILL LIBRARY
ACCEPTABLE USE POLICY

The primary use of public computer workstations and technology in L.P. Hill Library is for academic and research activities. Other non-restricted use such as entertainment is secondary and may be restricted when interfering with the primary use. Use of the Library network along with use of any of the campus network is a privilege, not a right, associated with membership in the university community. The Library Network and some of the components that make up, or are attached to it, are the properties of the Commonwealth of Pennsylvania.

Anything in this policy will be superseded by any policy adopted at a later date by Cheyney University of Pennsylvania.

1. Any deliberate act that may seriously impact the operation of computers, peripherals or the network is prohibited. Such acts include, but are not limited to, tampering with the components of the system (removing or unplugging any device), plugging personal equipment into a Library device, blocking communication lines or interfering with the operational readiness of a computer.

2. No person shall knowingly modify in any way a program or diskette that the Library supplies for any type of use at its sites. Downloading of files for coursework or saving documents created on a disk is allowed.

3. No person shall knowingly run or install on any Library computers a program that could result in damage to a file, computer system, or the network. This includes and is not limited to computer viruses, Trojan horses, and worms.

4. No person shall attempt to circumvent data protection schemes or uncover security loopholes.

5. The following type of information or software cannot be placed on any Library computer system:

    a. That which infringes upon the rights of another person.
    b. That which is abusive, profane, or sexually offensive to the average person.
    c. That which consists of information which may injure someone else and/or lead to a lawsuit or criminal charge. Examples of these are: pornographic materials, libelous statements or destructive software.
    d. That which consists of any advertisements for commercial enterprises.

6. No person shall harass others by sending offensive messages of any sort as defined by existing Cheyney University code of conduct statements.

7. Use of Library computer workstations and the Library network must be related to a Cheyney University course, research project, work-related activity, or departmental activity. When Library workstations are not in demand for use in this activities it may be possible to use them for other activities at the discretion of Library Management.

8. Any network traffic exiting the Library and Cheyney University is subject to the acceptable use policies of the network through which it flows (NSFnet, SSHENET, etc.), as well as to the policies listed here.

Offenders may also be subject to criminal prosecution under federal or state law, and should expect the Library and University to pursue such action. Under Pennsylvania Law it is a felony punishable by a fine up to $15,000 and imprisonment up to seven years for any person to access, alter or damage any computer system, network, software or database, or any part thereof, with the intent to interrupt the normal functioning of an organization [18Pa.C.S.3933(a)(1)].

Computer Use Policy

Smith Library, Christopher Newport University

Introduction

This is an addendum to CNU's policies (Policies Regarding the Use of the University's Computing and Communications Systems) and specifically concerns Smith Library's computer and electronic resources. Please refer to the University's policies located on the Computer Center's web site at http://www.cnu.edu/cctr/policies.html, and click on "University Policies."

Smith Library's computerized resources include but are not limited to those in the:

- Reference area (online catalog, cd-rom databases, online databases and Internet access)
- Media Center (microcomputers and networked computers)

Acceptable Use of Library computers and Internet

All library patrons using library computers in Smith Library are responsible for using computer resources in an ethical and legal manner. Users must respect the intellectual and access rights of others--locally, nationally and internationally.

Acceptable use includes:

- Using computerized resources for educational and research purposes only.
- Limiting your time on computer workstations to the posted time limits when other patrons are waiting to use them.
- Respecting the privacy of others by not sending them unwanted email messages, misrepresenting them when sending email, or tampering with their accounts, files, or data.
- Using the Library's limited resources, such as paper, toner, disk space, and Internet bandwidth, wisely.
- Using the computers in the Media Center only if you are a CNU student, staff or faculty member. (Alumni are not eligible.)

Unacceptable use includes:

- Obstructing other people's work by consuming excessive amounts of system resources or by deliberately crashing any Library computer system.
- Attempting to damage or alter computer equipment or software configurations.
- Using the network for commercial activity or any activity that violates Smith Library's licensing agreements.

Copyright

U.S. copyright law (Title 17, U.S. Code) prohibits the unauthorized reproduction or distribution of copyrighted materials, except as permitted by the principles of "fair use." Users may not copy or distribute electronic materials (including software, electronic mail, text, images, sound, programs or data) without the explicit permission of the copyright holder. The user is responsible for any consequences of copyright infringement; the Library expressly disclaims any liability or responsibility resulting from such use. Similarly, if you make materials available for others to retrieve or use (via a World Wide Web server, postings to a USENET newsgroup, etc.), you must respect the copyright of the materials.

Consequences

If computer use results in disruption of Library services or in behavior inappropriate for an academic library setting, the Library Supervisor on duty reserves the right to end the session. Internet sessions may also be discontinued if time limits have been exceeded or if inappropriate applications are being accessed. If the patron refuses to comply with the Library Supervisor's request, the matter will be turned over to the University Librarian or the Campus Police.

The Internet provides access to a wide variety of materials. However, the Internet is an unregulated medium and contains material that may be offensive or inaccurate. The Library does not monitor, control or take responsibility for the information accessed through the Internet. It is the responsibility of the user (or parent/guardian) to consider the source and determine the reliability, appropriateness, and quality of the material found on the Internet. Parents or guardians have the sole right and responsibility for guiding their children's Internet sessions.

Software and information downloaded from any source, including the Internet, may contain computer viruses. The Library takes no responsibility for the loss of data or any damage to the patron's discs and/or computers that may result from using the Library's hardware or software. The hard drives of the Library's computers are periodically purged of files saved or software installed without permission.

Questions?

Any questions about this policy may be directed to the University Librarian's Office.

Approved 9/97

☞ Back to the Library Policies page.

Web site last modified January 2001

Policies and Procedures
Karl E. Mundt Electronic Information Policy

OFFICE OF RECORD: Karl E. Mundt Library
ISSUED BY: Director of Library
APPROVED BY: 01
EFFECTIVE DATE: 5/31/00

Karl E. Mundt Library Electronic Information Policy for Library Users

POLICY

1. Introduction

1.1. The Karl E. Mundt Library Mission statement:

The University Library exists as an archive of accumulated knowledge, a gateway to scholarship, and a catalyst for the discovery and advancement of new ideas. In fulfilling its obligation to provide knowledge to the University and the scholarly community at large, the University Library collects, organizes, and provides access to recorded knowledge in all formats. The Library Faculty initiates discussions and proposes creative solutions to the information challenges facing the University and the scholarly community. The University Library's faculty and staff actively participate in providing quality services, access, instruction, and management of scholarly information.

1.2. The primary purpose of this policy is to detail the rights and responsibilities of consumers of electronic information in the Library.

1.3. Given the rapid rate of change within the field of electronic information this document must be regarded as a work in progress. Revision will not only be necessary but desirable.

PROCEDURES

2. Underlying Principles

2.1. The principles of academic freedom apply in full to the electronic communications and information environment.

2.2. The DSU Mundt Library's Electronic Information Policy is part of the University's overall policy structure and should be interpreted in conjunction with other existing policies. Use of the Library's computing and networking services is governed by the policy statement provided in this document, other relevant University policies, and all applicable laws. Individuals using these services should be particularly aware of the policies which apply to discrimination, harassment and equal opportunity and those which apply to the appropriate use of university resources. These and other policies can be found in major University policy documents, including: DSU Policies and Procedures Manual, DSU Faculty / Staff Handbook and the DSU Student Handbook.

2.3. The conventions of courtesy and etiquette which govern vocal and written communications shall extend to electronic communications as well.

2.4. The use of computing and network services provided by the Library shall be subject to all State and Federal laws. Anyone caught tampering with software or intentionally trying to deface the software as well as hardware would be held responsible for the damages.

2.5. The DSU Mundt Library has developed certain procedures to assist patrons in the use of electronic information resources. These procedures are based on the following principles:

2.5.1. Library workstations are to be used for course-related activity, scholarly research, and other activities directly related to the educational, research and public service mission of the University.

2.5.2. Use of library workstations to access electronic services offered by the Library takes precedence over other activities.

2.5.3. Software installed by patrons for personal use should be removed at the end of the session.

3. Definitions

3.1. Our primary patron base is the DSU community (faculty, students, and staff) but Library facilities are open to the public, even while some services are restricted. This policy recognizes that there is a larger user community that is defined by University policy, consortial agreements and contractual obligations.

3.2. For the purposes of this policy electronic information is any electronic resource that is made available by the DSU Library or that is accessible through Library workstations.

3.3. A Library workstation is a workstation that is physically located in the DSU Mundt Library.

4. Content of Internet Resources

4.1. The DSU Mundt Library urges library patrons to be informed consumers and carefully evaluate information obtained via the Internet.

Library staff may be available to assist patrons in making judgments about the reliability or currency of certain types of Internet information sources, but may not be able to provide definitive analysis of particular sources due to the extremely large variety and volume of information available via the Internet.

4.2. Most resources available via the Internet and other electronic information networks are "global" rather than "local" resources. The DSU Mundt Library does not and can not control the information content available through global resources such as information obtained from outside sources via the Internet. Internet resources enhance and supplement resources that are available locally within the library. The following should be kept in mind when evaluating information obtained via the Internet:

4.2.1. Information obtained via the Internet may or may not be accurate and reliable and may or may not be obtained from a reliable source.

4.2.3. Links to information on the Internet may not always be valid, and particular information sites on the Internet may sometimes be unavailable and this unavailability often occurs unpredictably.

4.2.4. Certain information obtained via the Internet may be considered controversial by some library patrons.

5. The DSU Mundt Library is not responsible for damages, indirect or direct, arising from a library patron's use of electronic information resources.

6. Library Patron's Rights

6.1. Library patrons have the right to confidentiality and privacy in the use of electronic information to the extent possible, given certain constraints such as proximity of other patrons and staff in public settings, security weaknesses inherent in electronic communications, and the library's need to conduct periodic use studies.

6.2. Library patrons have the right of equitable access to electronic information networks in support of the educational, research, and public service mission of the University, subject to the constraints of equipment availability.

7. Library Patrons' Responsibilities

7.1. Library's electronic resources are distributed via the DSU campus network. Therefore, all use of library-provided network connections falls under the campus-wide policy of computing, network access and use. The DSU Mundt Library requires that library patrons using electronic information networks such as the Internet do so within the guidelines of acceptable and responsible use.

7.2. Acceptable and responsible use of Library computing and communications facilities and services requires that you:

7.2.1. Respect the legal protection provided by copyright and license to programs and data.

7.2.2. Respect the rights of others by complying with all University policies regarding intellectual property.

7.2.3. Respect the rights of others by complying with all University policies regarding sexual, racial and other forms of harassment, and by preserving the privacy of personal data to which you have access. Users shall take full responsibility for messages that they transmit through the Library's computers and network facilities.

7.2.4. Respect the privacy of others by not tampering with their files, tapes, passwords, or accounts, or representing others when messaging or conferencing.

7.2.5. Demonstrate common courtesy by not disrupting others or overusing system resources or equipment.

7.2.6. Use only computer IDs or accounts and communication facilities which you are duly authorized to use, and use them for the purposes for which they were intended.

7.2.7. Respect the integrity of computing systems and data; for example, by not intentionally developing programs or making use of already existing programs that harass other users, or infiltrate a computer or computing system, and/or damage or alter the software components of a computer or computing system, gain unauthorized access to other facilities accessible via the network.

7.2.8. Use Library computing and communications facilities in a manner which is consistent with the ethical principles set forth by the University and with accepted community standards.

7.2.9. Respect and adhere to any State of South Dakota or Federal laws which may govern use of these computing and communication facilities.

8. Breach of Policy

8.1. Violations of any aspect of this policy may result in the temporary or permanent loss of privileges as determined by the DSU Disciplinary Board. They are treated like any other ethical violation as outlined in University policy documents, including, but not limited to, DSU Policies and Procedures Manual, DSU Faculty / Staff Handbook and the DSU Student Handbook.

9. Rules of Use – <u>Public Access</u> Workstations

9.1. The following information will be posted at the publicly accessible workstations:

9.1.1. <u>These workstations are to be used for research purposes only</u>.

9.1.2. Absolutely <u>NO</u> personal email, chat rooms, or game playing.

9.1.3. Individuals not affiliated with Dakota State University may be limited to fifteen (15) minute use periods.

9.1.4. Individuals not affiliated with Dakota State University are asked to pay for their printing at the front desk at the price of $.05 per page.

9.1.5. All children under 12 must be supervised by an adult.

These workstations are to be used for research purposes only.

PLEASE

<u>NO</u> personal email, chat rooms, or game playing on these machines.

Individuals not affiliated with DSU may be limited to 15 minute use periods.

All children under 12 must be supervised by an adult.

Printing: Individuals not affiliated with DSU are asked to pay for their printing at the front desk at the price of $.05 per page.

Sign sample for public, not electronic classroom, workstations.

Return to Policies and Procedures Page

Last updated 10/04/2000

Use of Library Computers
March, 2000

In an effort to make library computers more readily available to Earlham students, employees and their families, we are instituting new policies for Lilly and Wildman. These policies will go into effect on Wednesday, March 29.

LILLY

(1) The computers in the Lilly reference lab area are restricted to use by Earlham students, employees and their families.

(2) The computers in the Lilly reference lab will have a screen saver that requires a password. Earlham students, employees and their families can obtain the password from a staff member. Please do not divulge this password to others.*

(3) The four computers near the Lilly main entrance will not have a screen saver that requires a password. These computers are available for non-Earlham patrons of the library.

WILDMAN

(1) The computers in the Wildman Science Library are restricted to use by Earlham students, employees and their families.

(2) The computers in the Wildman Science Library will have a screen saver that requires a password. Earlham students, employees and their families can obtain the password from a staff member. Please do not divulge this password to others.*

(3) The computer near the Wildman main entrance will not have a screen saver that requires a password. This computer is available for non-Earlham patrons of the library.

---

* The use of this screen saver and password applies only to computers in the library and not those in the Computer Labs which are on the lower levels of Lilly and Wildman

Fitchburg State College

Library Policy
Acceptable Use POlicy

By using this computer you agree to abide by the acceptable use policies & rates of *Fitchburg State College* and the FSC Library including the following:

- ✓ Use of this computer is restricted to educational and research purposes.

- ✓ Personal e-mail communication on this computer is not permitted.

- ✓ Use of this computer for gaining, chat, or web site design is not permitted.

- ✓ Out of courtesy to other patrons please restrict your use of this computer to one (1) hour per session.

- ✓ Available services include: CD-ROMs, Online Databases, and Library Catalog. Double-click on the icon for the subject you wish to research.

MIS Acceptable Use Policy

www.fsc.edu/mis/AcceptUse.htm

Copyright by Fitchburg State College

James A. Rogers Library
Computer Use Policy

Francis Marion University
Florence, SC 29501-0547

The primary purpose of Francis Marion University is to make available "to people of all ages and origins an excellent undergraduate education in the liberal arts and selected professional programs." The University also "strives to provide the Pee Dee region of S.C. with a variety of educational and cultural enrichment services." The primary purpose of the James A. Rogers Library is to support the educational curricula of the University and to support general research in the Pee Dee region. Therefore, public access computers in this library are provided primarily for the use of students, faculty, and staff at Francis Marion University. Persons from the community may use the computers for research and/or educational purposes. The following restrictions apply to users of public access computers in the Library:

- Violation of United States or South Carolina State law including copyright laws and licensing agreements is unacceptable.
- DOWNLOADING OF TEXT FILES, SOFTWARE, EXECUTABLE FILES, DATABASES, AND SIMILAR "LIVE" TECHNOLOGY TO COMPUTER HARD-DRIVES IS PROHIBITED.
- Though not expressly forbidden, recreational use of the Internet is discouraged. Users engaging in recreational e-mail may be asked to move should the terminals be needed by faculty, staff, and students for research purposes.
- THE LIBRARY PROHIBITS CHAT ROOMS.
- THE LIBRARY PROHIBITS GAMES.
- The Library staff may monitor the usage of any public access computer in the library.
- Downloading of computer viruses is prohibited.
- Modification or destruction of library hardware, software or data including display and desktop configurations is forbidden.
- Harassment of other library users including the display of graphics which may be reasonably interpreted as offensive is unacceptable.
- Attempted evasion of system and network security measures is prohibited.
- The library reserves the right to impose time limitations on the use of library computers.
- The library assumes no responsibility for damage, direct or indirect, arising from the use of its computer and network facilities.

INTERNET RESOURCES

- It is the sole responsibility of the user to determine the accuracy and completeness of information obtained through the Internet.

- Internet resources may contain material of a controversial nature. The library does not control access to or content of material on the Internet.
- Although the library Web page identified specific links as starting points for Internet research, the library cannot control Internet access points because of the rapid and unpredictable changes of Internet addresses.

VIOLATIONS

- Library patrons in violation of any portion of this policy will be advised of the appropriate section and asked to comply.
- The library reserves the right to terminate network access for users who continually violate stated policies.

- - - Policy subject to change without notice - - -

Library Information/Services and Policies

Library Home Page

Library Internet Policy

Furman University Libraries

The purpose of library computing resources is academic research. Priority in the use of computers is given to Furman students, faculty and staff. Use of computing resources is subject to compliance with University regulations and all applicable laws. Harassing, discriminatory, illegal and/or unethical behavior is expressly prohibited.

Use Priorities

- The purpose of library computers is academic research by Furman students, faculty, and staff. This is the highest priority for use.
- Secondary uses of library computers include academic research by persons not associated with the university and non-academic use by Furman students, faculty, and staff. These are medium priority uses.
- Use of library computers for purposes other than academic research by persons not associated with the university is not authorized. All use in this category is by definition low priority, and patrons may be required to cease these activities at any time.

Patrons should offer to give up their seats to accommodate higher priority uses and may be required to by library employees.

Electronic Messaging

Electronic messaging includes e-mail, chat, and posting notices to electronic bulletin boards. Furman students, faculty, and staff may use electronic messaging from library computers but this is not considered a library function. Use of electronic messaging is not authorized by patrons not associated with the university.

There are several activities that are expressly prohibited as inappropriate use of electronic messaging at Furman, including:
- Unprofessional, harassing, discriminatory, illegal and/or unethical behavior. Activities for commercial gain or personal profit.
- Forgery of messages, hacking, or otherwise breaking into someone's files or stealing their password.
- Downloading of copyrighted materials without proper consent.
- Origination or forwarding of "chain letters," defined as any letter sent to several persons with a request that each send copies to several persons with the same or similar request.
- Any activity that significantly prevents or inhibits the conduct of university academic or administrative work.

For campus-wide policies on electronic messaging, see Policy File 072.1.

Viewing Objectionable Material

No limitations will be placed on the Internet content that Furman University students, faculty, and staff may view for the purposes of research in conjunction with classes or other scholarly activity. If a patron is viewing Internet content which might be considered objectionable (including but not limited to obscene, pornographic, or hate group sites), a library staff member may inquire as to the status of the patron and the purpose of the activity. If the library staff member determines that the patron is not associated with the university or is not conducting scholarly research, then he or she may ask the patron to cease that activity, to cease using library computers, and/or to leave the library. Patrons are required to comply with these requests. If a patron does not comply, Public Safety will be contacted and disciplinary or legal action may be taken.

Use of Library Computers by Minors

Parents should note that Furman University is a community of adults, and the library provides unfiltered Internet access to serve the needs of that community. Minors using the library may encounter materials that might be considered objectionable on the Internet as well as in the stacks. The library takes no responsibility for the exposure of minors to objectionable materials in any format. Parental accompaniment to the library and guidance in the use of library resources is recommended.

Enforcement of Policies by Library Staff Members

All library faculty and staff members shall have the right and authority to enforce these policies at their discretion. If a library employee believes that any person is violating any of these policies, he or she may ask the patron to cease that activity, to cease using library computers, and/or to leave the library. Patrons are required to comply with these requests. If a patron does not comply, Public Safety will be contacted and disciplinary or legal action may be taken.

Authorized university personnel may, at the request of the appropriate university officials, assist in the investigation of prohibited activities by examining or providing the contents of electronic messages stored in or passing through any equipment or system owned by or under the control of the university for any purpose at any time.

For campus-wide guidelines on confidentiality of electronic communications, see Policy File 078.2.

LAWRENCE UNIVERSITY | ABOUT LU | ADMISSIONS | ACADEMICS | NEWS | LIBRARY | MUSIC | INFO

THE LIBRARY

Mudd Library Public Computer Acceptable Use Policy

The public access computers in the Lawrence University Library are available for **scholarly research and educational purposes only**. These computers are provided primarily for the use of the students, faculty, and staff of Lawrence University, and for public use of the United States Federal Depository Library Program Electronic Collection (as provided in Section 1911 of Title 44, USC). Fox Valley community members may use the computers for **scholarly research and educational purposes**, although at busy times, preference will be given to members of the Lawrence campus community. The following additional restrictions apply to all users of public access computers in the Lawrence University Library:

- The Library public access computers may not be used for **financial transactions, chat, email, games or other recreational use.**
- The Library reserves the right to restrict access to, and/or impose time limitations on the use of Library computers.
- The Library reserves the right to limit the use of Library printers.
- Harassment of Library staff or other Library users, including the display of graphics in a manner which may be reasonably interpreted as offensive, is unacceptable.
- The Library assumes no responsibility for damage, direct or indirect, arising from the use of its computer and network facilities.
- The Library assumes no responsibility for use of the Internet by minors. The Library has no control over information or images that minors might access. External web pages may be offensive to some; supervision is the responsibility of the parent or guardian.
- Modification or destruction of Library hardware, software or data including display and desktop configurations is forbidden.
- Unauthorized access to computing resources or accounts, or attempted evasion of system and network security measures is prohibited.
- Violation of United States or Wisconsin state law, including copyright laws and software licensing agreements is prohibited.
- Library staff will monitor the use of Library public access computers.

Violators of the above will be asked to stop. Continued violation by

BACK

TO TOP

CONTACT

students will result in filing of charges with the Honor Council and/or Judicial Board, as appropriate to the circumstances. Continued violation by persons not affiliated with Lawrence University may result in loss of library privileges. Campus Security will be contacted as appropriate.

SITE GUIDE | SEARCH | FOR LU STUDENTS | FOR FACULTY & STAFF | FOR ALUMNI | FOR THE MEDIA

LIBRARY COMPUTER USE POLICY

1. Maryville students, faculty, staff and Friends of the Library have priority.

2. Computer use is limited to 20 minutes per person when others are waiting. Please be considerate of others waiting to use the computers. One computer per person.

3. Printing is free up to 10 pages. After 10 pages, the cost is $.10 per page. Please pay at the circulation desk. Downloading to disk and E-mailing documents is available from most databases.

4. Word processing, spreadsheets and other office software products are not available on these computers. They are available at campus computer labs.

5. You may access your email from these computers under the following conditions:
    a. There are available computers
    b. No one is waiting to use a computer for library research
    c. You may be asked to give up a computer to someone who needs it for research if there are no other available computers

Revises 2/01

Reeves Library Computer Policy

The limited computers in Reeves Library are available primarily for research. This includes accessing the library homepage to search databases, indexes and abstracting services, and other Internet resources.

When not in use for research, computers may be used to access email, to use other campus resources such as Blackboard, and to work on documents using library resources.

The library computers are not available for use in chat groups, real-time conversations, any instant messenger service, or long-term usage of any kind. Please take advantage of the computers in the Student Computer Lab in Monocacy Hall for paper writing or extended use.

Use of a library computer may be limited to one half hour.   Research activities must take precedence over other uses.

Reeves Library
March 14, 2001

Reference Room Workstation Use Policy

Library

Catalogs

Resources

Research

Services

Help

The Reference Room workstations are provided for Otterbein College students, faculty and staff with access to library catalogues, databases and other information resources to help them meet the objectives of their studies, research or job-related tasks.

This policy is to set out appropriate use of the Reference Room workstations to: ensure the maximum library-related use of limited numbers of workstations in the reference room; prevent damage to library computing resources; ensure Otterbein primary users to have enough access to the reference workstations.

Primary Users

Students, faculty and staff of Otterbein are considered primary users and will be given priority in the use of the workstations. A limit of 30 minutes will be enforced if other primary users are waiting.

Other Users

Community members, special borrowers and local high school students may use the workstations for educational purposes, but only during hours of low use when workstations are still available to primary users. Other users are limited to use no more than one hour per day while the school is in session. (You may be interrupted if workstation is needed by a primary user)

All users are asked to limit their search sessions to 45 minutes or less.

The following are library-related activities which are considered appropriate for use on the Reference Room Workstations:

1. Searching public catalogues, databases and files mounted by the library.

2. Searching public catalogues, databases and files of other institutions using the mechanisms provided by library.
3. Searching the Internet for study, research and teaching.
4. Capturing search results to disk, printer, e-mail, etc.

The following are non-library activities for which other college computing facilities should be used:

1. Use of personal e-mail. (E-mail, word processing, and printing services are available in the Academic Computing Center or in the library computer lab via the campus network)
2. Use of word processing, spreadsheets, and other workstation applications not explicitly listed on the workstation menus.
3. Posting to newsgroups, listservers and other networked resources.
4. Use of floppy disks except to download files.
5. Use of library workstations to access or complete online assignments.

Prohibited Activities

1. Use of the workstations which violates the college computer policy, such as destroying files; damaging equipment; removing memory chips, accessing confidential files, etc.
2. Tampering with or changing the workstation, components, or default setup.

Library users in violation of this policy will be asked to refrain from the restricted activity. Failure to comply will result in removal from the library.

Last modified on December 08, 1999
Comments & suggestions: *webmaster@otterbein.edu*
Copyright © 2001 by Otterbein College, Westerville, OH 43081-2006
Otterbein Web *Disclaimer*

LAVERY LIBRARY
PC USAGE POLICY

- The computers in Lavery Library are primarily intended for online research by the Fisher community.

- Patrons using email, MS Office Suite, or chat services may be asked to temporarily forfeit use of a computer for a patron waiting to do online research.

- Patrons are encouraged to keep printing to a minimum and to copy to diskette or zip disk, or email results when possible.

PRINTING GUIDELINES

Free printing is a courtesy.
- PRINT ONLY one copy of a document; photocopy others.

To conserve paper and toner:
- PRINT ONLY information required for academic use.
- PRINT ONLY the pages you need.
- COPY to diskette or zip disk if possible.
- EMAIL documents to your account when possible.

11-2000

3690 East Avenue • Rochester, New York 14618 • 716-385-8000

Policies > computer use

Public access computers (PCs only) are located on both levels of the library. All of the workstations have internet access and are intended for library research only. Inappropriate use of the library computers (Internet Relay Chat, Instant Messaging, Napster, etc) ,may result in the suspension of library borrowing privileges.

There are local, dot-matrix printers attached to each of the library computers. Library users may print to these printers free of charge. Additionally, each public access computer is connected to a networked laser printer that is located in the library staff office area. Users may print to the laser printer for a fee of 5 cents per page.

Users may download files to disk if they wish. All of the PCs are equipped with 3.5" disk drives, and most are equipped with 100MB Zip Drives

There are no word processing or spreadsheet applications on the library computers. Students must use one of the student computer labs in order to use these software applications.

Library users may not load their own software onto the library computers

Any misuse or abuse of library computers may result in the suspension of library borrowing privileges.

UNIVERSITY OF GREAT FALLS LIBRARY
POLICY ON PUBLIC ACCESS TO COMPUTERS AND NON-STUDENT COMPUTER USE

This policy is designed to promote responsible, ethical, and secure public use of the University Library's electronic computer facilities. The library is committed to providing high quality service to patrons in accordance with the institution's Computer Network and Internet Access Policy and the American Library Association's Library Bill of Rights. The library's electronic resources, which include networked and non-networked databases and Internet access, are intended for use by current university students, faculty, and staff. As a courtesy, community patrons and alumni are also allowed to use these systems. **Current students, faculty, and staff have priority.**

All users are expected to conform with the University's Computer Network and Internet Access Policy which prohibits the misuse of electronic resources by: a) gaining unauthorized access to remote computers; b) running or installing programs which could result in damage to files or University systems; and c) attempting to circumvent data protection schemes.

Public computers will **not** provide access to the UGFNet e-mail system or administrative and academic computing facilities. The library provides Internet access to informational and educational resources, but strictly prohibits the use of its electronic facilities for word processing, e-mail, chat rooms, MUDS, MOOS, or gameplaying. Patrons are limited to one 30-minute Internet session per day.

To preserve paper, patrons should download information onto a personal floppy disk whenever possible. Files downloaded by patrons are done so **at their own risk**. The library provides a laser printer for use with its electronic resources. After the first five pages, printouts are 5¢ per page.

DISCLAIMER

The University Library staff does not monitor or control materials on the Internet and cannot be responsible for Internet content. The University Library staff does not censor access to materials or protect patrons from Internet-based information which may be personally offensive. Children are not permitted to use Library computer systems unless a parent is present at the workstation.. It is the responsibility of parents to supervise and restrict their child's access to Internet information.

1 October, 1997

MANTOR LIBRARY INTERNET USE POLICY

Internet use in the Library is intended primarily for research purposes which will take precedence over all other activities.

The Internet is currently an unregulated medium. Unlike other library resources, it is not organized, cataloged, or indexed. The information on the Internet includes much that is personally, professionally, and culturally enriching. It also provides access to material that may be offensive or disturbing to some individuals, as well as access to information that may be factually incorrect and/or illegal.

Mantor Library does not monitor and has no control over the information available through the Internet, and specifically disclaims any warranty as to the information's accuracy, authoritativeness, timeliness, usefulness or fitness for a particular purpose. Mantor Library endorses the Library Bill of Rights, including the most current interpretation on electronic access, as adopted by the American Library Association, and supports the democratic principle of every citizen's right to free access to information. (Copies of the Library Bill of Rights are available at the Access Services Desk and Reference Desk, also on the Web at http://www.ala.org)

Parents/Guardians concerned about their children's use of electronic resources are ultimately responsible for setting standards and establishing guidelines for their children. Mantor Library affirms the responsibility of parents to determine the appropriateness of Internet-accessed resources, and all other library materials, for their children.

Internet use will be managed in a manner consistent with other Mantor Library service policies. Misuse of the computer or Internet access may result in the loss of computer privileges. Reference staff can provide limited assistance for basic start up procedures. Books and periodical articles may be available in the Library's collection to answer specific Internet-related questions.

Please see guidelines on other side.

University of Maine at Farmington

Use of the Internet and Mantor Library Computers

Mantor Library has guidelines for the use of its electronic resources by the public. These guidelines include, but are not limited to, the following:

- Mantor Library computers are to be used primarily for research purposes, such as locating books, journals, or Internet sites that are for classes or informational purposes.

- During times of heavy use, time on computers may be limited to 30 minutes for all machines.

- not support, nor offer assistance with personal email, chat rooms, Usenet groups, and other functions not directly related to a patron's academic research.

- The Library does not provide diskettes for downloading files and is not responsible for any loss or damage to personal disks.

- Patrons must use only Library-supplied software; patrons may not use personal software or alter or attach equipment to the Library's hardware.

- Patrons will be charged a nominal fee for the use of certain consumable supplies such as paper consistent with the Library's mission.

- Unacceptable uses include, but are not limited to:

  ‣ harassing other Library or computer users or staff.

  ‣ libeling others.

  ‣ intentional exposure to other individuals of material or images which they (or their parents/guardians) may find personally unsuitable.

  ‣ attempting unauthorized access to files, data or passwords.

  ‣ disruption or unauthorized monitoring of electronic communications.

  ‣ unauthorized copying of copyright protected material.

  ‣ violating, or attempting to violate, computer system security and/or software license agreements.

  ‣ damaging or attempting to alter computer equipment.

  ‣ incurring any costs to Mantor Library.

UNIVERSITY OF
SOUTHERN COLORADO
UNIVERSITY LIBRARY

Home   Search   Forms   Tour   Catalog   Electronic Resources   Help

COMPUTER USE POLICY

Computer equipment and software must be used as installed. Users are not permitted to add, delete, or modify the installed hardware or software.

Any user abusing, misusing, or engaging in any use of computer equipment or software not authorized by the University or the Library, or intentionally introducing a virus will be prohibited from using reference computers.

Users may be liable if they permanently or temporarily damage any equipment or software. Cases will be referred to the University Police if the damage is significant or deemed to have been intentional.

Use of a single computer is limited to a maximum of two persons at one time unless a class assignment necessitates larger groups at one terminal.

Use of the computer terminals can be limited to 15 minutes if people are waiting or if a reservation system is in effect. Library staff will notify users when time limits are in effect.

Orders for printing are limited to the time the user remains at the terminal. Users must cease issuing print orders 15 minutes before library closing time. Users must pay 10 cents per page for computer printouts before leaving the reference area.

Reference computers may not be used for any type of word processing or personal data processing. Users will be directed to computer laboratories on campus for these activities.

Librarians will have the right to ask Campus Police to respond should major disputes arise between users as to who has the right to use a terminal. The librarian-in-charge of the library has the right and the authority to ask any person to vacate the terminal and/or the library if deemed necessary.

Peterson Memorial Library
About Us   Off-Campus Access   Services   Other WWC Libraries

Library | College Place

Catalog

Reserves

Online Databases

Full-text Resources

Internet Resources

Other Libraries

POLICY FOR ACCEPTABLE USE OF PUBLIC ACCESS COMPUTERS AND THE INTERNET

Peterson Memorial Library provides access to electronic resources which serve the educational, research, curricular, and service needs of Walla Walla College students, faculty, staff, and administration. Resources are provided via the College's local area network or the Internet and include electronic library catalogs, online databases received by the library, free Internet databases, and other relevant material. These resources are provided within the context of the **Library's** and the **College's** mission statements.

PRIMARY USERS

Walla Walla College students, faculty, staff, and administration have first priority for academic and work-related research. Secondary use, such as browsing the Web for personal interests within reasonable, ethical, and legal constraints, is permitted. Users may be asked to surrender a workstation to a primary user who needs to do research. Members of the wider community may use the computers during periods of low demand. Parents and legal guardians are responsible for minors' use of library resources. A person violating library policy may be asked to leave the building. At all times, the Library reserves the right to restrict access to its computer workstations.

INTERNET RESOURCES

The Internet contains a broad range of material which may include sites containing additional and legitimate academic resources which enhance the library's collections. However, the Internet is an unregulated environment over which the library has no control. Users may also find inaccurate, incomplete, biased, outdated, inappropriate, offensive and/or illegal material. Therefore, each individual must be a discriminating information consumer, always evaluating the information they find on the Internet. Consistent with the library's **Collection Development Policy**, library personnel have selected and made available on a **Library Web Page**, links to a variety of sites identifying starting points for research. However, the Library does not take responsibility for any material listed on this page or accessed from the Internet.

RESPONSIBLE USE

Users are expected to employ electronic resources in an efficient, ethical, and lawful manner. They are also expected to operate within the framework of the **College's Responsible Computing Policy**. Freedom to access and display information is constrained by the rights of others, in addition to Federal and State law. Library personnel may request a user to remove images or text from the screen of a workstation if, in their judgement, the image or text could be offensive to others. Persistent violations of library policy could result in loss of library privileges. Users who need to access questionable sites for legitimate research should make arrangements with a reference librarian. The user is responsible for observing copyright law, avoiding plagiarism, and for evaluating material for accuracy, timeliness, and appropriateness.

UNACCEPTABLE USES

All uses that are illegal, commercial in nature, or hamper the academic mission of the college are prohibited. Such activities include, but are not limited to:

- Chat-rooms, E-mail or other messaging tools, games, etc.
- Accessing personal network accounts
- Viewing, displaying, or downloading suggestive, threatening, harassing, or racist material
- Monopolizing workstations for secondary use when others are waiting
- Commercial use, including online shopping
- Making illegal copies of software (see Colleges Copyright Policy [link])
- Loading any hardware or application of program software onto library computers
- Violating copyright laws or software licensing agreements
- Destruction of library equipment
- Noncompliance when asked by library personnel to desist an activity or leave the library

Home - About - Off-Campus Access - Services - Other WWC Libraries - WWC

Contact Us   Search

Voegel Library is open to the general public for study and research. Wartbrug students, faculty, and staff engaged in educational activities have priority in the use of college computers.

We ask members of the general public:

- To use library computers for research purposes only and not for electronic mail, chat rooms, games, or sexually explicit materials;

- To limit the amount of time they use library computers, especially during busy periods;

- To print no more than one copy of materials, and to copy only materials essential to their research; and

- Not to use other campus computers.

The library staff reserves the right to limit or to deny service to anyone who is unwilling to abide by these guidelines.

Library Appropriate Computer Use Policy

All patrons must follow the Winona State University Appropriate Use of Computing Policy located at:
http://www.winona.msus.edu/tsc/appropriate_use_of_computing.htm

Access
The Winona State University Library does not limit access to materials or attempt to prevent users from viewing materials that some individuals may find offensive.

Individual Responsibilities
The information found on the Internet is provided from around the world. Not all of that information is accurate, up-to-date, legal or acceptable to all individuals. The library does not control the Internet and, therefore, cannot be held responsible for its content. Individuals who use the Internet are responsible for evaluating the validity and appropriateness of the information they access.

WSU Library Main Page
The WSU library main page was designed and is maintained by the librarians. The library assumes responsibility only for the information provided on its pages.

The library's pages also feature links to other sites. In choosing sources with which to link, librarians follow the library's policies and guidelines (as an example, see http://www.winona.msus.edu/library/acq/buk.htm for the book selection policy). The library has not participated in the development of these other sites and does not control these sites. Links are not endorsements and the library assumes no responsibility for these sites.

Guidelines for Use of Computer Facilities
Library staff may limit the number of patrons using the same terminal.
Before patrons leave terminals, they are requested to close all programs and restore all settings.
Patrons may:

> not change computer desktops or start ups;
> not save files on hard drives;
> not shut off computers;
> not install programs;
> not damage computer equipment or software;
> not engage in harassing or defamatory activity on-line;
> not use terminals for illegal activity.

Other
Since most printing is provided by student fees, patrons are requested to use restraint in printing. All printouts should be picked up.

State and federal laws may apply to the use of computers for transmission and duplication of information. Library patrons may not access illegal materials through library facilities.

Minors must request permission to use the library's computer facilities. Permission may be granted for uses such as searching for government documents or working on a high school project.

Unlawful activities will be reported to WSU Computer Information Services, university security or the Winona Police Department. Violation of university or library computer use policies will be dealt with on an individual basis. Violation may result in the loss of library computing privileges.

If there are resources that are available on only select computers, and those computers are in heavy demand, the librarian may use his or her discretion to five the patron a time limit for use of a computer. If computer resources are insufficient for demand, a librarian can impose time limits for computer use for patrons.

The station behind the Reference Desk is the research station. Under normal conditions, this station is to be reserved for a librarian to conduct reference interviews or to set a patron up on an online resource for extended assistance. That station will be the computer designated for special, single IP services. If a patron needs on e of the services only available on that machine, the librarian can ask other patrons to relinquish it.

Schmidt Library Workstations: Acceptable Use Policy

Schmidt Library workstations are provided to support the educational mission of Schmidt Library and York College of Pennsylvania. Members of the York College community and visitors are expected to use Library workstations in a responsible, ethical manner.

Any use of these workstations must be consistent with the **Mission** of the Library and the College, the **York College of Pennsylvania Information Systems Policy Statement**, the **Code of Conduct** as described in the **York College Student Handbook**, and any relevant federal or state laws.

By using **Library workstations**, you accept the following conditions pertaining to:

1. Use of the workstations
2. Use of the Schmidt Library web pages
3. Use of the Internet by minors
4. Liability

Use of Schmidt Library workstations

Workstations in Schmidt Library are provided for educational and informational uses only. Members of the YCP community have priority use of the workstations. Library staff may ask patrons who are making inappropriate or unreasonable use of a workstation to relinquish it.

Use of the Schmidt Library web pages

Responsible, ethical use includes the following:

- using the web for educational, informational, or recreational purposes (Using the web pages for commercial or illegal activities is not permitted.)
- identifying yourself clearly and accurately in any electronic communication
- respecting the privacy of others
- respecting the right of others to be free from harassment, libel, slander, or misrepresentation
- refraining from recreational use of text or graphics that can reasonably be construed as obscene
- respecting the security of this and other systems
- respecting copyright and intellectual property rights

Use of the Internet by minors

Schmidt Library assumes no responsibility for use of the Internet by minors. Schmidt Library has no control over information or images that minors might access. External web pages may be offensive to some; supervision is the responsibility of the parent or guardian.

Liability

Schmidt Library is responsible only for the content of pages bearing its name. Users are responsible for any outside Internet sites they reach; they are free to exit any offensive sites. Users are also responsible for evaluating resources for accuracy, currency, and authority. Schmidt Library assumes no liability for use of outside resources.

Send comments or questions about this page to **cybrarian@ycp.edu**.

Computer Usage Policy

- Print name (first and last) **clearly** and enter **accurate** sign-in time **clearly.**

- **Time limits:** 30 minutes are guaranteed; longer time depends on demand.

- You are expected to vacate your station within 5 minutes after being notified.

- Computers are to be used for research related activities and preparation of class assignments. Campus "Computer Use and Abuse Policy" idle computer "chatting," and viewing of offensive material and graphics.

30 minutes are guaranteed by signing up for computer.
Do not install or download software onto this computer.
Campus "Computer Use and Abuse Policy" forbids engaging in "unauthorized and time-consuming recreational game playing," idle computer "chatting," and viewing of offensive material and graphics.

APPROPRIATE USE DOCUMENTS

Institutional AUPs

Information Technology Services

Home

Activate your Account

Connect to Email

Contact Us

Network Status

Web Boards

Policy for the Use of Computing Facilities at Alfred University

Responsible Use of Computing Resources

The computers and networks at Alfred University provide students, faculty and staff with powerful tools for communicating with others and for supporting our educational mission. When used appropriately, these tools can significantly enhance your experience at Alfred. Unlawful or inappropriate use, on the other hand, can infringe on the rights of others and may result in judicial proceedings and the suspension or loss of computing privileges.

The fundamental guiding principle for the use of computing resources at Alfred is respect for the rights of others.

A. **User ID and Password Confidentiality:**

   1. Users are responsible for safeguarding their User IDs and Passwords.

   2. Never, ever, share your User ID or Password with anyone.

   3. Never, ever, use anyone else's User ID or Password.

   4. Users are responsible for anything sent or created using their User ID and Password.

   5. Users may not disguise or falsify their identity when using University resources and networks.

B. **Expectation of Privacy:**

   1. Alfred University computer users can expect reasonable confidentiality in the messages they receive and the files they create. Information Technology Services personnel do not routinely monitor an individual's computer use, nor do they routinely examine files or read electronic mail in an individual's account, or review any content on web pages accessible through the University's website. However, Information Technology Services staff is

responsible for responding to alleged abuses and has the right to investigate suspected offenses, to suspend or revoke computing privileges, or to remove or deny access to any content it deems objectionable or illegal.

2. System administrators have the right, but not the obligation, to monitor system and network activities to ensure optimal performance and integrity.

3. The Internet and email are public forms of communication. You should be aware that there is always a possibility that what you send via email or make available on a web site may be seen by unauthorized individuals. With this in mind we strongly urge you not to send or post anything that you wouldn't want to see on the front page of your hometown newspaper.

C. **Prohibited Activities:**

1. Unauthorized access:

- Users may not access (e.g. read, copy, alter, or delete) anyone else's files, electronic communications, backup tapes, floppies, printouts, etc. without specific authorization from that user.
- Users may not try to access another user's account or attempt to guess or "crack" someone's User ID or Password.

2. Interfering with the activities of others:

- Users may not modify, disable, or tamper with any files, software programs or equipment (computers, furniture, printers, manuals) provided by Alfred University, or attempt to bypass security measures in place on the University system or the resources to which it connects.
- Academic work takes priority over personal and recreational use in computer laboratories and the libraries.

3. Harassment: Users may not use University resources to send material that is fraudulent, profane, obscene, intimidating, threatening, defamatory, abusive, offensive, or otherwise unlawful or inappropriate.

4. Unauthorized use:

- Users may not use University computing resources or networks for personal gain, commercial or profit-making purposes unless specifically authorized to do so by the appropriate University official.

- Users may not use University resources or networks for political campaigning, personal statements or unauthorized solicitation.

5. Wasteful or frivolous use: Any wasteful or frivolous uses of computing facilities and resources are prohibited. Examples of such uses include, but are not limited to, the following:

- Chain mail – chain mail usually contains phrases such as "pass this on," "forward – don't delete," "don't break the chain," etc. Don't fall for it; don't forward it, it is chain mail.
- Mass mail – inappropriate use of mailing lists is considered a misuse of resources. Individual students are not authorized to send any mass emails. Recognized student organizations, faculty and staff may use mass mailings only for topics that meet the administrative or academic mission of the University. See Mass Mail Policy.
- Email bombing – email bombing is flooding someone's email with large email messages or large volumes of mail. It can disrupt service for all users and impact innocent bystanders.
- Virus hoaxes – virus hoaxes on the Internet are widespread. Before warning others about a virus, check its authenticity with the Helpdesk @ 607-871-2222.
- Creating unnecessary network traffic, for example, chain mail, spamming, network scanning or probing.

5. Illegal use: Examples of illegal uses include, but are not limited to, the following:

- Illegal copying – contrary to popular belief, materials found on the Internet, including text, digital images, trademarks, videos and digital audio files (e.g. MP3 format) are typically protected by copyright. You should always have permission to use any material you did not create. "Fair use" of web-related copyrighted material may be allowed under certain circumstances. Librarians at Herrick or Scholes Libraries can assist you in determining "fair use."

Special note regarding digital music and sound recordings on the Internet: The Recording Industry Association of America (RIAA) takes the unauthorized use of music and sound recordings on the Internet very seriously. They have developed a website at http://www.soundbyting.com to educate the public about copyright laws as they relate to music on the Internet. The bottom line is that sound recordings are typically protected by copyright, and copyright infringement (including unlawful uploading and downloading of music files) is against the law. Penalties are stiff (up to $250,000 in fines).

- Software piracy – software is protected by copyright law and unlawful copying of software is illegal. For more detailed information see Guide To the Ethical Use of Software.
- Tapping phone or network lines.
- Forgery – sending email in someone else's name.
- Child pornography – uploading or downloading this material is a federal offense.
- Distribution of pornography to minors.
- Obscenity – may not be used in mail headers, process names, personal/organizational web pages or any other output on University-owned computers or systems.
- Bomb threats and hoaxes – it is illegal to send a message via email that threatens other persons or property. Federal authorities may investigate these messages.

D. **Enforcement:**

Abuse of Alfred University computing resources and networks, or behavior that violates University policy or local, state or federal laws may result in temporary or permanent suspension of computing privileges, disciplinary action by the University and/or liability under applicable civil or criminal laws.

Information Technology Services reserves the right to prohibit unauthorized activities that disrupt network services.

Abuses and infringements under the Alfred University Responsible Use of Computing Resources Policy should be reported to the Associate Vice President for Information Services, the Assistant Director of Information Technology Services, or the Information Technology Services Helpdesk @ 607-871-2222.

Questions/Comments?

AU Homepage | AU @ a Glance | Academics | Admissions
Alumni | Parents | Faculty & Staff | News | Athletics
Research & Outreach | Student Life | Info Technology

Appropriate Use of Computer Resources

At Arkansas Tech University

Policy No. 1-99

Introduction

The University's computer and information network is a continually growing and changing resource that supports thousands of users and systems. These resources are vital for the fulfillment of the academic, research and business needs of the University community. Their use is provided as a privilege. In order to ensure a reasonable and dependable level of service, it is essential that each individual faculty member, staff member, and student must exercise responsible, ethical behavior when using these resources. The University does not censor internet content. Therefore all information on the Internet is available to any authorized users. Although we recognize the importance of this freedom we expect users to exercise reasonable efforts to privately view information that may not be suitable or appropriate for all groups. Misuse by even a few individuals has the potential to disrupt University business, and, even worse, the legitimate academic and research work of faculty and students.

This policy outlines the application of the principles that govern our academic community in the appropriate use of University computer and information network resources. Because it is impossible to anticipate all the ways in which individuals may misuse these resources, this policy focuses on a few general rules and the principles behind them.

This policy applies to the entire user community (e.g., all faculty, staff, students, alumni and retirees) of the University and to the use of any and all Arkansas Tech University owned or managed computer-related equipment, computer systems, and interconnecting networks, as well as all information contained therein.

Use of Resources

All users are expected to utilize Arkansas Tech University resources in a responsible manner consistent with Arkansas Tech University policies and the guidelines and operating policies that the Associate Vice President of Information Technology may issue from time to time. You are expected to take reasonable measures to ensure that traffic entering the Arkansas Tech Network from other networks conforms to this policy. Conversely, you are expected to take similar measures to avoid situations where traffic from the Arkansas Tech Network violates the policies of connecting networks.

The unauthorized use of resources is prohibited and, in many cases, may be in violation of the law. We are guided by the law in noting that unauthorized use includes, but is not limited to the following types of activities.

Harassment or threats to specific individuals, or a class of individuals:

1. Transmitting unsolicited information that contains obscene, indecent, lewd or lascivious material or other material which explicitly or implicitly refers to sexual conduct.

2. Using e-mail or newsgroups to threaten or stalk someone.

3. Transmitting unsolicited information that contains profane language or panders to bigotry, sexism, or other forms of prohibited discrimination.

Interference or impairment to the activities of others:

1. Creating, modifying, executing or retransmitting any computer program or instructions intended to: (1) obscure the true identity of the sender of electronic mail or electronic messages, such as the forgery of electronic mail or the alteration of system or user data used to identify the sender of electronic e-mail; (2) bypass, subvert, or otherwise render ineffective the security or access control measures on any network or computer system without the permission of the owner; or (3) examine or collect data from the network (e.g., a "network sniffer" program).

2. Authorizing another person or organization to use your computer accounts or Arkansas Tech Network resources. You are responsible for all use of your accounts. You must take all reasonable precautions, including password maintenance and file protection measures, to prevent use of your account by unauthorized persons. You must not share your password with anyone else or provide access to Arkansas Tech Network resources to unauthorized persons.

3. Communicating or using any password, personal identification number, credit card number or other personal or financial information without the permission of its owner.

Unauthorized access and use of the resources of others:

1. Use of Arkansas Tech University resources to gain unauthorized access

to resources of this or other institutions, organizations, or individuals.

2. Use of false or misleading information for the purpose of obtaining access to unauthorized resources.

3. Accessing, altering, copying, moving, or removing information, proprietary software or other files (including programs, libraries, data and electronic mail) from any network system or files of other users without prior authorization (e.g., use of a "network sniffer" program).

4. Making unauthorized copies of copyrighted materials. You should assume all software, graphic images, music, and the like are copyrighted. Copying or downloading copyrighted materials without the authorization of the copyright owner or that does not fall within the parameters of the "Fair Use" exceptions provided by law is against the law, and may result in civil and criminal penalties, including fines and imprisonment.

Use of University provided electronic storage.

1. Students and faculty will be provided with a user storage space in their home directory of the Domain Server "U:\Username ". The size of this space will be determined by the University based on the availability of space. This area should be considered a temporary storage location and is not intended for storage of critical files.

2. This area is not to be used as a storage location for any copyrighted materials to include, but not limited to, MP3, Expanded Music Waves, Movie Files or any other files that may have a copyright.

3. This area is not to be used to store files that may be considered Hacker Files (Sniffers, Crackers, Password Breakers, Monitors, Etc...)

4. The storage area needs to be cleaned out at the end of each semester and summer (I/II).

5. Files located in this area may be monitored to assure compliance with this and other University Policies.

6. This storage is provided at the discretion of the University and may be altered or removed completely at any time without notice. The University is not responsible for any file loss or corruption

Damage or impairment of Arkansas Tech University resources:

1. Use of any resource irresponsibly or in a manner that adversely affects the work of others. This includes intentionally, recklessly or negligently (1) damaging any system (e.g., by the introduction of any so-called "virus", "worm", or "trojan-horse" program), (2) damaging or violating the privacy of information not belonging to you, or (3) misusing or allowing misuse of system resources.

2. Use of Arkansas Tech University resources for non-University related activities that unduly increase network load (e.g., chain mail, network games and spamming).

Unauthorized commercial activities:

1. Using Arkansas Tech University resources for one's own commercial gain, or for other commercial purposes not officially approved by the University, including web ads.

2. Using Arkansas Tech University resources to operate or support a non-University related business.

3. Use of Arkansas Tech University resources in a manner inconsistent with the University's contractual obligations to suppliers of those resources or with any published University policy.

Violation of city, state or federal laws:

1. Pirating software, music and images.

2. Effecting or receiving unauthorized electronic transfer of funds.

3. Disseminating child pornography or other obscene material.

4. Violating any laws or participating in the commission or furtherance of any crime or other unlawful or improper purpose.

When Inappropriate Use of Computer Resources Occurs

The use of Arkansas Tech University resources is a privilege. The resources have always been, and will remain, the property of the University.

It is your responsibility to promptly report any violation of this computer use policy. In addition, you are requested to report any information relating to a flaw in or bypass of resource security to abuse@mail.atu.edu.

Reports of unauthorized use or misuse of the resources will be investigated pursuant to standard Arkansas Tech University procedures. All illegal activities may be reported to local, state or federal authorities, as appropriate, for investigation and prosecution.

While Arkansas Tech University desires to maintain user privacy and to avoid the unnecessary interruption of user activities, the University reserves the right to investigate unauthorized or improper use of University resources. This may include the inspection of data stored or the review of transmitted data on the network identified during the routine monitoring of the physical storage areas and network traffic, or once probable cause for the inspection had been established by other means. In the event that use is determined to be contrary to University policy or applicable law, appropriate measures will be taken. These measures may include, but are not limited to, permanent or temporary suspension of user privileges, deletion of files, disconnection from the Arkansas Tech Network, referral to student or employee disciplinary processes, and cooperating with the appropriate law enforcement officials and government agencies.

Arkansas Tech University is not responsible for information, including photographic images and musical recordings, published on or accessible through personal web pages, including personal home pages. The University does not monitor the contents of these personal web pages.

The individual or group creating or maintaining personal web pages is solely responsible for the content of the web page and may be held civilly and criminally liable for the materials posted on the web site. University guidelines for creating and maintaining web pages may be found on the Information Technology web page.

Information on Applicable Laws and Statutes

All users of the Arkansas Tech University computer and information resources are expected to be familiar with and to abide by University codes and policies, as well as local, state and federal laws relating to electronic media, copyrights, privacy, and security. A discussion of these laws and their relationship to the appropriate use of University resources may be found on the Information Technology web page.

Questions Relating to This Policy

The examples of unauthorized use set forth above are not meant to be exhaustive. Answers to frequently asked questions (FAQ) about the appropriate use of Arkansas Tech University computer and information network resources can be found on the Information Technology web page (http://technology.atu.edu/). Additional questions about this policy or of the applicability of this policy to a particular situation should be referred to Technology.Director@mail.atu.edu The Associate Vice President for Information Technology is the focal point for questions concerning appropriate use of University resources. Whenever you are in doubt regarding an issue of questionable use, it is strongly advised to resolve the issue before pursuing any questionable use of University resources.

(original signed by)

William E. Harmon

September 27, 1999

Revised April 21, 2000

Print out a AUCRP signature page

Aurora University Computer Use Policy

Computers have become an essential tool in higher education for instruction, research, and public service. Aurora University is committed to providing a wide range of high-quality computing services to students, faculty, and staff and to support the mission of the University as set out by the governing board. The following policies have been established to ensure the security and integrity of the University's computing resources and the fair and equitable access to those resources by all the members of the University community. These policies apply to all University computing systems (desktop, laboratory, and networked), and all hardware, software, data, and telecommunications devices associated with these systems. Failure to abide by these policies may result in the loss of computing privileges, reimbursement of damages, and possible disciplinary action.

1. **Authorized Use**. Access to Aurora University computing resources is available to faculty, staff, and all currently enrolled full-time and part-time students. Access may also be extended to others in support of educational and community service activities in the Aurora University service area. Students who have completed at least six hours of credit in the last year at Aurora University but are not currently enrolled may continue using their accounts until the end of one additional term. Accounts that have not been accessed for 120 calendar days will be deemed inactive and removed from the system.

2. **Distribution of Resources**. The utility of the University's computing services depends on the balanced distribution of limited resources. All users are expected to assist in the conservation of these resources and to avoid excessive system usage, connect time, and disk storage. Specifically prohibited is the use of the network for recreational activities that place heavy load on scarce resources, the creation or distribution of electronic "chain letters," and other types of use that would cause congestion of the network or otherwise interfere with the work of others.

3. **Disruptive Activities**. Any deliberate attempt to tamper with, disrupt, delay, or endanger the regular operation of the University's computing resources is prohibited. The creation or propagation of computer worms or viruses, or the distribution of electronic mail or software intended to replicate or do damage to another user's account or to University hardware, software or data is considered vandalism and will be treated

as such.

4. **Commercial Activity**. The University's computing resources are reserved for instructional purposes and the professional activities of its faculty and staff. The use of these systems for personal business or commercial use, such as the posting of commercial web pages and the distribution of unsolicited advertising, is prohibited.

5. **Property Rights**. All computer programs and files, unless they have been explicitly placed in the public domain by their owners, are private property and may not be copied or distributed without authorization. The users of Aurora University computer resources are subject to applicable laws governing intellectual property and should be aware that the copying, distribution, or use of protected material without proper permission or license is prohibited.

6. **Privacy**. Rights to privacy on the part of members of the Aurora University community extend into the computing environment. Prohibited activities include the following: accessing or attempting to access another user's computer account or files without specific authorization; the deliberate, unauthorized attempt, through misrepresentation or any other mechanism, to access University computers, computer facilities, networks, systems, programs, or data; and the use of University computer resources to gain access to restricted databases. Electronic mail poses unique challenges to the right of privacy: although all users have the right to expect that their electronic mail messages will not be viewed by others, for a variety of reasons this is difficult to ensure, and users are urged to post email messages with the understanding that occasionally their messages may reach readers other than the intended recipients. Users should also be aware that authorized computer administrators may on rare occasions need to access users' accounts for purposes of system maintenance and resource management.

7. **Harassment and Fraudulent Behavior**. The sending of harassing messages or files to or about another person, interfering with the legitimate work of another user, the transmission and display of abusive or obscene messages, and the sending of messages under an assumed name or modified address or with the intent to obscure the origin of the message is a violation of this policy and such activity may also be subject to applicable state and federal laws.

8. **Freedom of Expression**. The free exchange of ideas is central to the educational process. The Aurora University computer use policy supports this principle, with the exception of uses that violate the law, endanger computer resources, violate the policies articulated in this document, or are otherwise determined by University authorities to be inappropriate, unethical, or inconsistent with the educational goals of the university.

Approved by the University Assembly Oct. 10, 1997
Approved by Academic Council Oct. 24, 1997
Revised October 19, 2001

Aurora University
347 S. Gladstone Ave.
Aurora, IL 60506
(630) 892-6431
(800) 742-5281

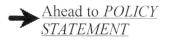

← Back to *APPENDIX B -- CODE FOR ETHICAL COMPUTER USE*   ↑ Up to *Table of Contents*   → Ahead to *POLICY STATEMENT*

INTRODUCTION

All members of the Bentley community, students, faculty, staff, and administration have opportunities to use computers and be affected by computer usage in the pursuit of their primary endeavors at Bentley College.

Therefore, it is critical that such computer use be performed in an ethical context which ensures that the use of these resources fosters the achievement of the individual user's goals, consistent with Bentley College's educational and research objectives.

Such an ethical context implies that computing resources will not be abused, wasted, or employed in such a way as to interfere with, or cause harm or damage to another person, institution, or company within or outside the Bentley College community. It is up to the individual to act responsibly in the use of computer hardware and software, data and computer outputs.

 **Copyright 1998 - Revised: 3/1999 - Contact: Webmaster**

← Back to *INTRODUCTION*

↑ Up to
*Table of
Contents*

POLICY STATEMENT

The fundamental purpose of the Bentley computer resource is to support an individual's primary endeavors as a student or employee of Bentley College.

An individual may only use accounts, files, software and computer resources authorized under his/her particular password.

Individuals must take all reasonable precautions (e.g., prevent unauthorized access to accounts or data by others) both within and outside the Bentley community.

Individuals must not make unauthorized copies of copyrighted software or data. An employee's questions of copyright provisions or permissions should be directed to his or her supervisor or the supervisor of the computing facility. A student's questions should be addressed to a member of the faculty or the supervisor of the computing facility.

Employees are expected to report to their supervisors or the supervisor of the computing facility, and students are expected to report to a faculty member or the supervisor of the computing facility, any violations, flaws or other deficiencies in the security of any and all Bentley College computer resources.

Individuals must not abuse the College's computing resources so as to reduce their efficiency to the detriment of other users.

Individuals must not attempt to modify system facilities, utilities, and/or configurations, or change the restrictions associated with their accounts, or attempt to breach the College's computer resources security system, whether with or without malicious intent.

Individuals must not use any network access provided by the College to affect other computers or the network in any of the above ways.

If uncertain about a specific situation, an employee should consult a superior or supervisor; a student should consult a member of the faculty before proceeding.

Violations of this policy will be handled in a manner consistent with comparable situations requiring disciplinary action.

Revised 3/29/93   **Copyright 1998 - Revised: 3/1999 - Contact: Webmaster**

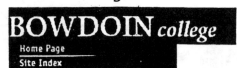

Computing & Information Services

CIS Computer Use Policy (revised 3/3/99)

The computing facilities at Bowdoin are provided for the students, faculty, and staff of the College. Users of the Bowdoin College computing facilities do so as guests of the College and are expected to conduct themselves accordingly. A user's right to continued use of the facilities is dependent upon compliance with this Policy. Bowdoin College is likewise a guest on the Internet, and use of the Internet through Bowdoin College facilities reflects upon the College. Responsible use requires that users not interfere with the normal and proper operation of the computing facilities or the Internet; not adversely affect the ability of others to use the college's equipment or services; and not conduct themselves in ways which might be harmful or offensive to others.

This Computer Use Policy governs the use of all computing equipment or facilities owned or operated by the College, including the use of the College's services or facilities via the Internet, dial-in modem, or other means. This document is posted in all public-computing spaces, sent to all students, staff and faculty members, and is available on the Computing and Information Services web site. All users of the College's computing facilities are required to comply with this policy, and by using the College owned facilities, agree to comply with it.

The College maintains facilities for archiving and retrieving data stored in user accounts. The College reserves the right to monitor any computer action or system record of any action that a user performs while utilizing the campus network. Users may expect privacy for all data stored in their accounts. Out of respect for personal privacy, the College does not examine the contents of files in user accounts except in response to user requests for assistance, or in extraordinary circumstances when system security or when trouble-shooting anticipated violations of this policy require it. Whenever the College determines that the contents of a user's file should be examined, an effort will first be made to notify the user and invite him or her to be present. However, if the system is under immediate threat, appropriate actions can be taken without prior notice to the user.

Although the College provides reasonable security against unauthorized intrusion and damage to data, the College does not warrant privacy or the integrity of stored data and reserves the right to examine data as described above. Communications over the Internet and even across the college's local campus network are not encrypted, and it would not be technically difficult for an eavesdropper to listen in. Also, e-mail messages in transit are stored as system files, and problems with the mail delivery system sometimes require that Computing and Information Services staff examine the contents of those files. The use of any hardware or software to access data that the user is not authorized to access, or to eavesdrop on the network is strictly forbidden.

To safeguard system security and enforce this policy, the Computing Center staff may limit or restrict any usage of the computing facilities, and may remove or otherwise alter any data, file, or system resources that may undermine the proper use of the system or violate the policy. Persons who abuse the computing facilities may also be subject to further disciplinary action by the College, in the same manner as violators of other College policies. In some cases, violators may also be liable for civil damages or criminal prosecution. The Director of Computing and Information Services administers this Policy. Appeals of the Director's decisions can be pursued through the Vice President for Finance and Administration. At the Director's discretion, any suspected violation of this Policy may be referred to the appropriate Senior Staff officer to initiate further disciplinary procedures.

Students, faculty and staff may create personal web pages on the College's web server, but a storage limit may be imposed. Contents of the web page can be of the user's own creation consistent with this Computer Use Policy. The College reserves the right to remove any portion of a web site which does not comply with the Policy.

[To Top]

Responsible Computer Use Includes the Following:

The specific restrictions listed below are not meant to be exhaustive; general College rules governing responsible behavior also apply. For example, obscene, false or harassing messages sent by computer or posted on a web site are just as unacceptable as obscene, false or harassing messages sent in any other medium, and normal College standards and procedures would apply in such cases.

1. **Respect for Other Users**

   A user's computer directories deserve the same consideration as his/her desk drawers. No user may access another user's files without permission, nor does the lack of file protection in itself constitute permission. The same respect should also be shown for other users' printer output. Persons with access to administrative data are obligated to keep it confidential.

   The system of accounts and passwords plays an important role in protecting the work and privacy of all users. You may log in only to your own account (except for extraordinary situations where faculty or staff receive a user's permission to access his or her account temporarily or where use of a group account has been approved by Computing and Information Services or an academic department).

   You may not use or attempt to discover another user's password, either locally or at a remote location.

   You are responsible for all use made of your account, and may not authorize anyone else to use your account (except as mentioned above). You must take all reasonable precautions, including password maintenance and file protection measures, to prevent its unauthorized use.

Unsolicited mailings to large groups are generally considered a nuisance and are not permitted. Policies are in place for the legitimate use of campus-wide mailing lists. These policies may be found on the CIS web site. Other examples of the inappropriate use of email include forging and chain letters.

2. Respect for System Availability and Integrity

Many users depend heavily on Bowdoin's computers to complete essential work. You may not damage any central or desktop system or misuse system resources to prevent yourself or others from doing work, nor may you write or run programs (often called "viruses") designed to do so, whether locally or remotely.

Due to restrictive software licensing agreements, the use of College owned computing equipment and resources is limited to educational purposes and college related professional activities. Bowdoin computing resources and facilities are not to be used for any non-college related commercial purpose, either non-profit or for profit. You may not maintain or use an account after withdrawing or terminating your status at the College, without approval from Computing and Information Services.

You must observe the specific rules governing the use of public computing facilities that are posted in each lab.

3. Respect for the Rights of Copyright Holders

Users must comply with all copyright and other applicable laws. Users should assume that all software, images and documents are protected by copyright unless they know otherwise.

Software is valuable property and is generally protected under copyright law. You may not copy protected software, including college-owned software, without a license or permission from the copyright holder, whether for your own use or for others. It is the user's responsibility to obtain the necessary license or permission or to determine that it has been obtained. Copying protected software and the use of illegally copied software are offenses subject to civil damages and criminal prosecution. Details about copyright may be found on the Library web site

Images and documents are valuable property and are generally protected under copyright law. Many images are frequently used in the creation of a web site. You may not copy any photograph, drawing, painting or any other image or document which is protected by copyright without permission of the copyright holder. Photographs used in Bowdoin College publications are protected under the photographer's copyrights. Please check with the Office of Communications or the College

Archives prior to the use of any Bowdoin photographs.

Policies Regarding the Use of the University's Computing and Communications Systems

I. Statement of Policy

This is a statement of policy regarding the use of CNU computer and communication facilities, including voice, data, and video. It relates to the use of telecommunications equipment (includecomputer networks internally and using the Internet) as well as mainframe, midrange, minicomputer, workstation, and personal computer systems. It, therefore, covers, all activities involving computing and communication facilities at CNU. Every user is expected to know and to follow this policy.

Every student is expected to know and to follow university policy in this area. The only activities not covered are those solely involving personal property which does not in any manner makeuse of access to internal networks or to the Internet or to any other equipment owned by the university.

II. General Purpose

University communication and computing resources are intended to support the educational, research, and public service missions of the university. All acceptable use of these resources must be in accord with the university honor codes and with this Student Handbook as well as relevant local, state, federal, and interactional laws and regulations.

1. Acceptable use must demonstrate respect for:
   - the rights of others to privacy;
   - intellectual property rights, (e.g., as reflected in licenses and copyrights);
   - ownership of data;
   - system mechanisms designed to limit access;
   - respect for others; and
   - individuals' rights to be free of intimidation, harassment, and unwarranted annoyance.

2. Policy towards Violations
   - CNU regards any violation of this policy as a serious offense (see Enforcement Regulations, below).

III. Use of information systems at CNU General Principles

Access to computer systems and networks owned or operated by CNU imposes certain responsibilities and obligations and is granted subject to university policies, and local, state, and federal laws. Acceptable use always is ethical, reflects academic honesty, and shows restrain in the consumption of shared resources. It demonstrates respect for individuals, intellectual property, ownership of information, system security mechanisms, and individuals' rights to privacy and to freedom intimidation and harassment.

Specific Guidelines for Acceptable Use
1. In making acceptable use of resources, you must:
- use resources only for authorized purposes;
- protect your user ID and the system from unauthorized use. You are responsible for all activities taking place under your user ID or that originate from your system;
- access only information that is your own, that is publicly available, or to which you have been given authorized access;
- use only legal versions of copyrighted software in compliance with vendor license requirements be considerate in your use of shared resources. Refrain from monopolizing systems, overloading networks, degrading services, or wasting computer time, connect time, disk space, printer paper, manuals or other resources.

Unacceptable Use
2. In making acceptable use of resources you must NOT:
- use another person's system, User ID, password, files, or data without permission;
- use computer programs to decode passwords or to access control information;
- attempt to circumvent or to subvert security measures;
- engage in any activity that might be harmful to systems or to any information stored therein, such as creating or propagating viruses disrupting services, or damaging files:
- use university systems for commercial or for partisan political purposes;
- make or use illegal copies of copyrighted software, store such copies on university systems, or transmit them over university networks;
- use mail or messaging services to harass or to intimidate another person; for example, by broadcasting unsolicited messages, by sending unwanted mail, or by using someone else's name or User ID;
- waste computing resources; for example, by intentionally placing a program in an endless loop, by using excessive amounts of paper through printing needlessly, frivolously, or for amusement, or by sending chain letters;
- use the university's systems or networks for personal gain; for example, by selling access to your User ID or to university systems or networks, or by performing work for profit with university resources in a manner not authorized by the university;
- publish Web pages that use or attach the university name to material that is not appropriate to the university's educational, research or service mission.
- engage in any activity that does not conform to the General Principles statement above.

IV.Protecting Electronic Access Privileges

1. General Policy Statement

The university is responsible for assuring the integrity of its computing systems. At the same time, the university strives to provide an open, accessible communications network in order to maximize the functionality and usefulness of these resources. The integrity of shared computing resources depends upon responsible behavior on the art of the users.

2. The Password or User ID

- Computing systems are protected by a system of electronic authentication and authorization procedures that rely on user passwords or user IDs for validation. It is the responsibility of all computing and network users in the university community to safeguard the access privileges granted to them.
- The owner of an access ID or user ID is accountable for its use. It is the ID owner's responsibility to protect the integrity of accessible systems and to preserve the confidentiality of accessible information as appropriate.
- Unauthorized electronic access is prohibited.
- Guidelines for managing your password
  - Passwords should be managed solely by the owner of the access ID.
  - Passwords should remain confidential.
  - Passwords should be changed periodically (e.g., at least once every 3 months) and at any time there is a reason to suspect a password has been compromised.
  - Passwords should follow guidelines issued by the granting agency of the university.
  - Passwords should never be displayed, printed, or otherwise recorded in an unsecured manner.

3. Reporting Suspected Security Breaches

- Anyone who has reason to suspect a breach of established security policy or procedure should promptly report it to the appropriate Dean, Director, Department Head, or to the Computer Center.

V. Enforcement Regulations

1. User responsibilities

All users of university computing resources are responsible for being aware of university policies governing computing and communications resources.

2. Minor infractions

Violations of these regulations will be referred to the University Disciplinary

Board, with a recommendation for disciplinary action subject to review and final action by the Dean of Students and a representative of either the Computer Center or the Department of Physics and Computer Science. If it is appropriate, cases may be referred to the honor board. Disciplinary action may range from university sanctions to recommendations for legal action. If the University Disciplinary Board finds that an offense may be in violation of the law, offenders may be prosecuted under the laws and regulations of the City of Newport News, the Commonwealth of Virginia, and the United States of America.

Student Computer Lab Use Policies:

Document Protection

- Our PC's operate at maximum capacity; therefore, it is crucial that you **save** your work often, especially before printing or spell checking.
- If your computer locks or crashes during document manipulation, seek a lab consultant immediately.

Consideration of Other Users

- Working in groups is allowed as long as the noise level is kept to minimum.
- Any displays of adult material will NOT be allowed on state computers.
  - **If found breaking this rule, you will be banned from the Computer Center labs.**

Computer Center Requirements

- Because the PC's are connected to an intricate network, the loading of software onto a machine is not allowed.
- Because all software is licensed only for use at CNU, you may not copy software for your personal use.
- The consultants will assist you with technical problems but will not aid in completing your homework assignment.
  - **Please consult your professor for help with homework or papers.**

- Given the high cost of printing, we request that you limit your print jobs:
- You may print ONE copy of your resume. You will have to make additional copies elsewhere.
- NOTE: If your print job does not print, DO NOT continue to send it to the printer.
  - Notify a consultant if printing is unsuccessful after the first attempt.

- Food and drinks are not permitted in the labs.
- Children are not permitted in the labs.
- For security reasons, the labs must close at the posted time.

State Requirements

The computers of CNU are property of the Commonwealth of Virginia. Therefore:

- Only state employees and students of state institutions may use our facilities.
- Only projects related to academia may be undertaken in the labs. Games are prohibited.

Clarion University Center for Computing Services

COMPUTER AND NETWORK USE POLICY

PURPOSE: To provide guidelines for the use and operation of computing systems, telecommunications facilities and network resources.

POLICY:

Clarion University of Pennsylvania computing, telecommunications, and networking resources are provided for the support of instruction, administration, and research activities of the institution. These resources are operated under a variety of security systems, procedures, and protocols. Use of these resources is a privilege granted by the University, with designated offices coordinating assigned activities. Users of these resources are expected to conduct their activities within the restrictions and overall university policies of Clarion University, the laws of the Commonwealth of Pennsylvania, and federal statutes. Misuse or improper use of Clarion University computing facilities, telecommunications and network systems or their associated facilities, resources and equipment include (but are not limited to) the following:

1. theft, damage or destruction of computing facilities, programs or data;
2. access, copying and/or modification of computing facilities, programs or data without proper authorization;
3. reproducing or allowing others to reproduce copyrighted software material in any form without proper authorization, or not in keeping with the University's copyright regulations or federal and state laws;
4. access or use of computing facilities, programs, or data which are not authorized to the user's account;
5. sharing access codes or any security-related procedures, files or accounts with other individuals;
6. interference with computer systems, telecommunications facilities, networks, or other resources including e-mail systems, such that the activities of other users are inhibited or disrupted (e.g. computer viruses);
7. intentionally rendering computer systems, telecommunications facilities, networks, or other resources inoperative (e.g. "crashing" the system or network);
8. use of computing systems, telecommunications facilities, networks, or other resources including e mail systems, for political activity or commercial use including (but not limited to) the promotion of "for profit" and/or privately owned businesses or sale of private property;
9. use of computing systems, telecommunications facilities, networks, or other resources including e mail systems to abuse, defame, harass or threaten another individual or group, commit fraud or distribute other unlawful messages;
10. excessive use of computer systems, telecommunications facilities, networks, or other resources for frivolous or non-productive purposes;
11. and all other unauthorized acts or uses of university computing facilities or resources, or any other actions not in accordance with university policies, or not in the best interests of Clarion University.

Clarion University of Pennsylvania will take appropriate action against a user who willfully misuses computer resources. Such actions may include (but are not limited to) canceling the user's account, revoking the user's operating privileges, revoking access to resources, assessing discipline in accordance with applicable university policy, and seeking prosecution under the laws of the Commonwealth of Pennsylvania or federal statutes.

The Center for Computing Services produces electronic backup copies of all of the contents and components of the central VMS cluster system, including the e-mail component, as part of the Clarion University Crisis Prevention and Recovery Program. These backup files are completed every evening and are stored for a period of up to five years. Current backup procedures do not capture messages deleted the same day they are received.

Violations of the computer use policy may be reported to the Center for Computing Services, G-1, Still Hall, x2280.

[Home Page | People Finder | Admissions | Academics | Student Life | Administration | University Libraries | Computing Services | Registrar | University Calendar]
Send your comments to Cindy Lauer

Concordia Computing

Computing News

Help Materials

Faculty Resources

Tech Facilities

Computing Policies

Who's Who

Computing Policies

Concordia College Policy on Access to Computers and Computer Software

The use of the Concordia College academic computing facilities is available at no direct charge to all faculty, registered students, and staff in support of the regular curricular function of the College. Users are expected to use this privilege in a manner consistent with the College policy on Academic Integrity. Specific guidelines include, but are not limited to:

- Assigned class work has priority over personal use of the facilities. Users doing recreational computing must relinquish their station if requested to do so by the lab consultants or Residential Life staff.
- Accounts must be used ONLY by the assigned user. Computer accounts should be kept secure by changing passwords frequently. Users are responsible for material originating from their account.
- Users must abstain from actions which waste computer resources, alter the configurations of college equipment, destroy the integrity of computer-based information, or compromise the privacy of users. Specifically prohibited are obscene or threatening material. Specific guidelines for personal Web pages are covered by the College Web Policy document.
- Manuals, disks, and supplies must not be removed from the labs.
- College-owned computing facilities may not be used for profit-making purposes.
- The use of the computer equipment, network account, or software of another member of the community without express permission is trespassing and an invasion of privacy. Other violations of authorial integrity, including plagiarism, invasion of privacy, unauthorized access, forging or sending anonymous mail, and software copyright violations, my be grounds for sanctions against members of the academic community.

Campus computer resources exist to fulfill the educational mission of the College. Computer Services reserves the right to monitor network account activity to maintain system security, or to investigate reasonable suspicion of policy violations. Users should not presume the privacy of electronic communications

Failure to conform to the above standards will be considered a violation of the Concordia Academic Integrity Code and/or Social Policy Code, and can lead to temporary or permanent suspension of computing privileges, and College disciplinary action.

See the Computer Code Violation and Enforcement Policy

Concordia Computing

Computing
News

Help
Materials

Faculty
Resources

Tech
Facilities

Computing
Policies

Who's
Who

Computing Policies

Ethical Use of Computers at Concordia College

Concordia College provides computer services for educational, research, and administrative purposes. Because computer resources are finite, access to the public labs and to the Internet is not a right, but a privilege, and that privilege is conditional on your abiding by the following guidelines.

Student, faculty, and staff use of computers is governed by the Academic Responsibility Code as reported in the *Directory* and *Faculty Handbook*. Further, *Academic Integrity at Concordia College: A Handbook for Faculty, Students, and Staff of the College* (1995) stresses the need for all members of the college community to be people of integrity. The ethical use of computer resources at Concordia College nurtures integrity by stressing *respect* for yourself, others, academic integrity, and computer resources.

Respect Yourself

--Protect your password, and change it often. Avoid obvious passwords, and do not write your password down. Use the *passwd* command regularly to change your password.

--Never allow another person to use your account. Any member of the Concordia community can have an individual account free of charge. Remember, you are responsible for all activity on your account.

--Always log off your account when you are done.

--Do not access material that is obscene or pornographic or promotes illegal behavior

Respect Others

--Never use the computers to send threatening, obscene, unwanted, or harassing material

--Never access anyone's account but your own or interfere with someone else's files

--Do not impede others's access to public computers by recreational computing (e.g., wantonly engaging the talk feature, playing games, or sending social email) while others are waiting.

--Never write or knowingly execute a program designed to alter or destroy other users's files (i.e., a virus program)

--Respect the Lab Consultants and follow their instructions, especially if you are asked to let another user have your station when you're using it for recreational purposes

Respect Academic Integrity

--Credit all material (e.g., text, images, codes, etc.) taken from the Internet or a cd-rom and used for academic purposes (e.g., reports, essays, presentations, etc.). Failure to do so is plagiarism.

--Never download or distribute a copyrighted program unless your licensing agreement specifically allows it

--Concordia's World Wide Web site is an official publication of the college. All materials posted to it must adhere to the Office of Communication's WWW guidelines.

--You have a responsibility to report and/or stop violations of the computer ethics code

Respect Computer Resources

--Do not use computer resources for commercial gain or frivolity

--Do not squander computer supplies, physically abuse computer equipment, or alter the configuration of college computers

--Do not use excessive disk space on *cobber*, *gloria*, or any of the public-computer hard drives

--Do not waste processor time by excessive use of the talk feature or playing games

--Minimize modem use

Concordia home page | **Computing home page**

Questions, comments to: landa@cord.edu

last modified: Saturday, February 10, 2001 06:01:33

Concordia Computing

Computing News

Help Materials

Faculty Resources

Tech Facilities

Computing Policies

Who's Who

Computing Policies

CONCORDIA COLLEGE COMPUTER CODE VIOLATION AND ENFORCEMENT POLICY

This policy describes the guidelines for handling violations of the Concordia College Policy on Access to Computers and Computer Software. It applies to all Concordia students, faculty, and staff. Complaints are investigated by the Academic Computing Coordinator. All warnings and correspondence are copied to the Director of Security and the Network Systems Manager. Violations are grouped into the following three categories:

Level 1 Violation: Users receive an e-mail warning and explanation of the violation, and a request that the activity not be repeated.

Common violations at this level include Policy violations such as sharing access to an account, complaints from other users of unsolicited mail or offensive material, and wasting of lab supplies.

Level 2 Violation: Users meet personally with Academic Computing Coordinator to discuss the violation, and receive a one to two week account suspension.

Violations at this level include a repeated Level 1 incident, or actions severe enough to disrupt network services.

Level 3 Violation: The user meets with Academic Computing, Student Affairs, and/or Campus Security. These are serious violations and the user may be charged with and Academic Integrity or Social Policy Code violation, and may have computer privileges indefinitely suspended.

Violations at this level include repeated violations at other levels, serious threats or harassment, and intentional interruption of network services or security.

Exception: Web policy violations result in immediate suspension of web publishing privileges and Level 3 enforcement because the Web is considered an official College publication and a public document.

Complaint Procedure: Complaints may be communicated in person, in writing, or by e-mail to the Academic Computing Coordinator, Student Affairs Office, or Campus Security Office. Users are also encouraged to communicate any concerns about proper use of the computing facilities to the e-mail address *stop-it@cord.edu*.

Users who feel they have been wrongly accused of computer policy violations may bring a complaint to the appropriate judicial board.

Culver-Stockton College
Student Computing Policy Agreement

PLEASE READ CAREFULLY

Every student using the college's telecommunications and computing equipment and capabilities agrees to abide by the tenets set forth in the following computing policy:

Culver-Stockton College students (referred to as I) hereby acknowledge that permission is granted to them for academic use of the computing and telecommunications facilities and services of the college, including its computer systems, associated peripherals and files, and telephone and network access, according to the terms described herein. In consideration of the permission granted to use the above mentioned systems, they hereby acknowledge that:

1. The college licenses the use of software from a variety of outside companies. This software and its accompanying documentation is to be used only in the college's office areas, classrooms, computing labs, and authorized residence hall areas and is not to be removed from such designated areas. I agree that I will not copy, disclose, transfer, reproduce, without written permission, any computer software or documentation the college licenses. I agree to abide by all terms of the of the college's license agreements, this policy statement, campus "Rules for Computer Use", ResNet policies, and applicable federal and state laws regarding college software and use of the college's computer and telecommunications equipment. According to United States Copyright law, any illegal reproduction of software is subject to civil damages of as much as $100,000 and criminal penalties, including fines and imprisonment.

2. The college's computer and telecommunications systems are not to be used in any way that diminishes or interferes with the use of those systems by others. I acknowledge the college's right to remove immediately any files which appears to be intended for any such misuse. I further acknowledge the college's right to inspect when necessary, as a function of responsible system management, all electronic files and other recorded information on the college's computing and telecommunications facilities.

3. I agree to be a responsible email user by refraining from sending messages deemed to be obscene, obnoxious, slanderous or fraudulent. I also agree to respect the college's equipment capabilities by not sending chain letters or other information of that type. I further agree not to use college email to sell personal items to students and faculty/staff on my mailing lists. To protect my account and my privacy I agree to keep my passwords private.

4. If I participate in the ResNet program I take full responsibility for my computer and any activities performed on that computer. This includes the actions of any person who has access to or been given permission to use my computer by myself. I acknowledge that any actions deemed inappropriate from my personal computer by myself or another person will result in, at the minimum, my residence hall connection being terminated.

5. I agree to include the following disclaimer on my default page on the Culver-Stockton College Web site. I also agree for personal and linked pages to be in good taste. Failure to do so will result in my web pages being discontinued.

    Disclaimer to be added to your default page on the Culver-Stockton College Web site:

    "The views and opinions expressed in this page and any linked pages are strictly those of the author. The contents of this page have not been reviewed or approved by Culver-Stockton College".

By utilizing the systems outlined in this policy statement, I agree to the terms herein, and shall indemnify and hold the college harmless against all damages, losses, expenses, or costs resulting from the breach of obligations contained herein. Furthermore, I recognize any violation of any of the above policies will result in the revocation of all Culver-Stockton College computer privileges, including network and internet access from college facilities or personal machines, and could also result in criminal prosecution.

Dated: August 17, 1999

Policies and Procedures
Computing Privileges

OFFICE OF RECORD: Computing
Services

ISSUED BY: Director of Computing Services

APPROVED BY: 03

EFFECTIVE DATE: 02-13-87   (Revised 5/

COMPUTING PRIVILEGES

SCOPE

Provide direction for the use of computing resources, associated with or accessible from Dakota State University, by faculty, students, staff, and others.

POLICY

The use of computers and related technologies, including hardware, software, and courseware, is a privilege. The Director of Computing Services is authorized to extend the privilege of using appropriate computing and related hardware, software, and courseware to persons who are either: members of the faculty, members of the student body, members of the staff, participants in workshops, short courses and similar approved activities and projects, members of an entity that has contracted for the use of computing resources, or teachers, administrators, or students of a K-12 school that has a working agreement with DSU for such services.

PROCEDURE

1. All persons who wish to use a computing service provided through Dakota State must agree to comply with the following rules:

    A. Users will not use another's user code or password.

    B. Users will not access the files of any other user without the prior consent of the other user. Authority to access, create, modify, or delete information contained in machine files must be granted explicitly. The capability to access does not imply the authority to access. Any willful unauthorized access of information is a violation of the ethical standards of Dakota State

University and may also be a violation of certain state or federal statutes.

C. Users will comply with all provisions of software or courseware copyrights unless a specific waiver is authorized by the President.

D. Users will utilize computing resources only for authorized administrative, educational, research or other scholarly activity, or a project approved by the Director of Computing Services.

E. Users will comply with all applicable laws.

F. Users will abide by the Educom "Ethical Use of Computing Resources" statement which has been adopted by Dakota State University. (See Attachment A.)

G. Users will abide by the Acceptable Use Policy of any network accessed through the University's computing and communications environment.

H. Users will exhibit appropriate behavior. Inappropriate behavior includes, but is not limited to:

- excessive playing of computer games; game players who are heavily utilizing computing resources during high usage times will be asked to cease using the computing resource.

- attempting to modify or remove computer equipment, software or peripherals without proper authorization.

- accessing computers, computer software, computer data or information, or networks without proper authorization, regardless of whether the computer used for access or the computer accessed is owned by the University.

- circumventing or attempting to circumvent normal resource limits, login procedures, and security regulations.

- using computing facilities, computer accounts, or computer data for purposes other than those for which they were intended or authorized.

- sending fraudulent computer mail, breaking into another user's electronic mailbox, or reading another user's electronic mail without permission.

- sending any fraudulent electronic transmission, included but not limited to fraudulent requests for confidential information, fraudulent submission of electronic purchase requisitions or journal vouchers, and fraudulent electronic authorization of purchase requisition or journal vouchers.

- violating any software license agreement or copyright, including copying or redistributing copyrighted computer software, data or reports without proper, recorded authorization.

- using the University's computing resources to harass or threaten others.

- taking advantage of another user's naiveté or negligence to gain access to any computer account, data, software, or file.

- physically interfering with another user's authorized access to the University's computing facilities.

- encroaching on another user's ability to make authorized use of University computing resources, including but not limited to:

  - sending excessive messages, including electronic chain letters
  - printing excessive copies of documents, files, data, or programs
  - modifying system facilities, operating systems, disk sub-directories, or operating environment
  - damaging or vandalizing University computing facilities, equipment, software or computer files.

- disclosing or removing proprietary information, software, printed output or magnetic media without the explicit permission of the owner.

- reading another user's data, information, files, or programs on a display screen, as printed output, or via electronic means, without the owner's explicit permission.

2. Charges for the use of computing services may be assessed by the Director of Computing Services with the approval of the President. Computing services supporting student instruction, faculty development, and DSU administration will normally be provided without charge. However, charges may be assessed for computing services in support of sponsored research; non-academic, personal, or consulting projects; and, contract or off-campus projects. Charges may include the costs associated with issuing the user a University Identification Card. The President may waive any charge for a particular individual or group of users.

3. Software available at Dakota State University includes copyrighted programs developed by Dakota State staff and programs licensed from a variety of vendors. It is expected that all faculty, staff, students and campus guests will use any software -- whether or not supplied by Dakota State University -- only in accordance with license agreements and copyright provisions applicable to the specific software package.

4. Dakota State faculty, staff and students who knowingly violate any software license agreement or copyright provision will be disciplined as described in #5 below. Such discipline shall not exempt the individual from applicable civil or

criminal remedies available through federal or state judicial proceedings.

5. Dakota State faculty, staff and students learning of any misuse of software or related documentation, unauthorized information access, or inappropriate behavior should immediately notify the Director of Computing Services, or a College Dean, or the Vice President of Student Affairs. Upon receiving a report of the misuse of the computing privilege, the member of the administration will:

  A. Take immediate steps to verify if there is misuse and ascertain the circumstances of the reported or observed incident.

    1. If the misuse or suspected misuse involves students, then the Director of Computing Services and the Vice President for Student Affairs should be notified immediately.

    2. If the misuse or suspected misuse involves faculty, staff, or off-campus personnel, then the Director of Computing Services and the Academic Vice President and Provost should be notified immediately.

  B. Assist the Director of Computing Services in preparing a report of the misuse or suspected misuse to the Academic Vice President and Provost and President within five (5) working days.

  C. The Director of Computing Services may immediately suspend the computing privileges of any person who makes inappropriate use of the computing resources of Dakota State University. A report of all actions associated with the suspension of computing privileges will be provided to the Vice President for Student Affairs in the case of student violations, and to the appropriate Executive Council member in the case of faculty or staff violations within two (2) working days of the suspension action. Within seven (7) working days the Vice President for Student Affairs or the appropriate Executive Council member must either initiate formal disciplinary proceedings or reinstate the computing privileges. To appeal a decision, students should refer to Policy 03-30-00, Appealing Academic and Administrative Decisions, and faculty/staff should refer to the Board of Regents Policy Manual 4:7(faculty), 4:8 (exempt) or 4:9 (CSA).

6. While use of the facilities is not restricted solely to faculty, staff, and students, the priority of user access varies depending on class schedules, user status and other factors. The following sections define those priorities and factors.

Facility Status

DSU Computing facilities are divided into two classes -- General Access Computing Facilities and Limited Access Computing Facilities. General Access Computing Facilities are available for use by all authorized users except when reserved for class usage. Limited Access Facilities are available to a specific subset of authorized users. A list of General Access and Limited Access Facilities is provided in Attachment B. This listing will be updated by Computing Services as changes occur.

Scheduled Classes

Classes scheduled through the Registration and Academic Records Office take priority over all other usage of general access computing facilities. Regular class schedules will be listed on the boards outside each computing lab at the beginning of each semester. It will be the user's responsibility to check the scheduled class hours and vacate the lab prior to the time class is scheduled. One-time use and special classes are scheduled through the College office. Whenever possible, such usage will be posted in advance. In all cases, non-participating users may be asked to vacate the lab when activities scheduled through the Academic Records Office or the College office are in progress.

General Access

Any General Access Computing Facility that is not scheduled for a class is available for general access during regular posted hours of operation. During periods of general access, the following rules and priorities apply.

- Registered Students and Workshop Attendees
  Persons registered/enrolled in a class/workshop scheduled by the University have priority over other users. In the event that all computers are occupied, any user that cannot display a valid DSU identification may be asked to move or cease using the computing facilities at the request of a user with a valid student ID. Normally the group sponsoring the workshop is expected to schedule sufficient computing time to meet the needs of enrollees.

7. All users of the computing facilities must comply with all pertinent DSU policies, including the Computing Privileges policy (#03-61-00) and the Use of University Facilities policy (#01-75-00). Of particular importance are those policies concerning copyright and smoking. The use of DSU computing facilities by any individual whose sole purpose is to make a profit is prohibited--except for those exceptions outlined in the Use of University Facilities policy (#01-75-00).

Attachment A
ETHICAL USE OF COMPUTING RESOURCES

Dakota State University, along with many other colleges and universities, supports this statement from the 1989 brochure "Using Software", distributed by EDUCOM*:

"Respect for intellectual labor and creativity is vital to academic discourse and enterprise. This principle applies to works of all authors and publishers in all media. It encompasses respect for the right to acknowledgment, right to privacy, and right to determine the form, manner, and terms of publication and distribution.

"Because electronic information is volatile and easily reproduced, respect for the work and personal expression of others is especially critical in computer environments. Violations of authorial integrity, including plagiarism, invasion of privacy, unauthorized access, and trade secret and copyright violations, may be grounds for sanctions against members of the academic community."

University employees and students are required to adhere to any specific conditions or restrictions required by the licensing agreements for software programs purchased with University funds. For commonly used licensing agreements, the following conditions apply:

1. It is illegal to copy a software application program and install that single program for simultaneous use on multiple machines.

2. Unauthorized copies of software programs may not be used on University equipment. This applies even though you yourself may not have made the illegal copy.

3. Purchase of the appropriate number of copies of a software program is necessary for maintaining legal status, especially if you are using machines connected to a network.

4. University employees and students are prohibited from assisting in making or using illegal copies of software.

5. University employees and students are permitted to make an archival (back-up) copy of a software program provided it is not used or transferred separately from the original program.

*EDUCOM is a non-profit consortium of over 450 colleges and universities.

Attachment B
General Access and Limited Access Computing Facilities

General Access Computing Facilities
Beadle Hall
General Access Laboratory - BH-113
East Hall
General Access Laboratory - EH-306
General Access Laboratory - EH-300 (Macintosh LC Lab)
Karl Mundt Library
Library Lab - main floor
Kennedy Center
General Access Laboratory - KC-123
Controlled Access Laboratory - KC-124
Science Center
General Access Laboratory - SC-114
Sioux Falls Facility
General Access Laboratory (Consistent with the policy on Use of DSU Facilities

Sioux Falls)

Limited Access Computing Facilities

Beadle Hall

The Hunter Laboratory - BH-110

Kennedy Center

BIS Lab - KC-116

Residence Halls (Emry, Higbie, Richardson, Zimmermann)

Residence Hall Labs

Residence Hall Rooms

Sioux Falls Facility

BEI Laboratory

University Faculty and Administrative Offices

Return to Policies and Procedures Page

Last updated 5/20/98

Electronic Policy

About Emerson

Admission

Alumni

Directories

Financial Aid

News Releases

Opportunities

Student Life

Search

Site Map

Emerson College
Electronic Information Policy Guidelines
for Responsible and Ethical Behavior
Version 2.12 (October 16, 2000)

(This statement draws heavily upon the following documents: Ithaca College's Campus Wide Information Service Policy Statement, Bentley College's Computer Ethics Policy, SIPB Guidelines for Appropriate Use of MIT's Campus Wide Information Services, University of Michigan's Computing Handbook, University of Missouri-Columbia Code of Conduct for Legal and Ethical Computer Use, University of Rochester's Acceptable Use Policy and User Manual, University of California - Santa Barbara's Responsible Use Policy and Harvard's Use of Computers and Networks.)

All students, faculty and staff are encouraged to choose computing resources appropriate to their work. All users of Emerson College's computing resources are expected to behave in a responsible, ethical, and legal manner. In general, appropriate use means respecting the rights of other computer users, the integrity of the physical facilities, and all pertinent and contractual agreements.

The following list, though not exhaustive, provides some specific guidelines for responsible and ethical behavior:

* Use only computers, computer accounts, and computer files for which you have authorization.

* Network services and wiring may not be modified or tampered with. This applies to all network wiring hardware and jacks.

* Network services and wiring may not be extended beyond the port provided. Retransmission or propagation of network services is prohibited without explicit permission. This includes the installation of hubs, switches and wireless equipment.

* You are ultimately responsible for anyone's use of your network connection.

* Obey established guidelines for any computers or networks used inside and outside the College.

* Do not attempt to access restricted portions of the operating system, security software, or accounting software unless authorized by the appropriate College administrator.

* Abide by all applicable laws.

* Respect the privacy and personal rights of others. Do not access or copy another user's electronic mail, data, programs, or other files without permission.

* Abide by all applicable copyright laws and licenses. Both College policies and the law expressly forbid the copying of software that has not been placed in the public domain or distributed as "freeware" or "shareware." Reproduction of copyrighted material is subject to the Copyright laws of the United States (Title 17, U.S.C.). Infringement of copyright may subject persons to fines and penalties.

* Employ appropriate standards of civility when using computer systems to communicate with other individuals.

* Be sensitive to the needs of others, and use only your fair share of computing resources. The network is a shared resource, thus network use or applications which inhibit or interfere with the use of the network and services by others are not permitted.

* Treat computing resources and electronic information as a valuable College resource. Protect your data and the systems you use.

* Use Emerson's computing facilities and services for College related work.

Emerson College

Activities that would jeopardize the College's tax-exempt status are prohibited. Persons are not permitted to engage in consulting or other business ventures using the Emerson College network.

* The network may not be used to provide computer services or Internet access to anyone outside of Emerson College for any purposes without the express written permission of the Vice President of Administration and Finance.

* Stay informed about the computing environment.

* Take due precaution against the spread of computer viruses. Install virus protection software on your computer. Regularly check hard drive and exposed floppy disks for the presence of viruses.

* The following activities are specifically prohibited: disclosing your password to others; using somebody else's password to gain access to Emerson's system; using illegally obtained software on the system; copying, altering or deleting someone else's files without that person's permission; forging messages; cracking passwords and systems; sending harassing or threatening messages; The sending of unauthorized anonymous messages; the sending of bulk unsolicited messages; reading someone else's files without permission system attacks; denial of services; and other malicious uses of the network and systems.

* Sending data over the campus network and/or Emerson College computer systems and identifying yourself as anything but your assigned username is strictly forbidden.

* Network connections may not be used to monitor network traffic or devices by means of hardware or software applications.

* All IP addresses, both static and dynamic, are the Property of Emerson College.

Violations of Guidelines

Violations of the above policies are considered unethical and may lead to College disciplinary action and/or criminal prosecution. Individuals are encouraged to report information concerning instances in which the above guidelines have been or are being violated. In accordance with the established College practices, policies, and procedures, confirmation of inappropriate use of Emerson College technology resources may result in termination of access, expulsion from the College, termination of employment, legal action or other disciplinary action.

Questions about this document and reports of possible violation can be directed to the EIP Executive Board (send a message to EIPB@emerson.edu).

About Emerson | Admission | Alumni | Directories | Financial Aid | News Releases | Opportunities | Student Life |

Search | Site Map | Comments for Webmaster | Copyright 1998 Emerson College All rights reserved

DRAFT

Fort Valley State University
COMPUTER AND NETWORK USAGE POLICY

"Respect for intellectual labor and creativity is vital to academic discourse and enterprise. This principle applies to works of all authors and publishers in all media. It encompasses respect for the right to acknowledgment, the right to privacy, and the right to determine the form, manner, and terms of publication and distribution. Because electronic information is volatile and easily reproduced, respect for the work and personal expression of others is especially critical in computer environments. Violations of authorial integrity, including plagiarism, invasions of privacy, unauthorized access, and trade secret and copyright violations, may be grounds for sanctions against members of the academic community." The EDUCOM Code.

1.   BACKGROUND AND PURPOSE

This document constitutes a University-wide policy intended to allow for the proper use of all Fort Valley State University computing and network resources, effective protection of individual users, equitable access, and proper management of those resources. This should be taken in the broadest possible sense. This policy applies to Fort Valley State University network usage even in situations where it would not apply to the computers in use. These guidelines are intended to supplement, not replace, all existing laws, regulations, agreements, and contracts which currently apply to these services.

Campus units that operate their own computers or networks may add, with the approval of the unit head, individual guidelines which supplement, but do not relax, this policy. In such cases, the unit must inform their users and the Director of Computing and Information Systems prior to implementation.

Access to networks and computer systems owned or operated by Fort Valley State University imposes certain responsibilities and obligations and is granted subject to University policies and local, state, and federal laws. Appropriate use should always be legal, ethical, reflect academic honesty, reflect community standards, and show restraint in the consumption of shared resources. It should demonstrate respect for intellectual property; ownership of data; system security mechanisms; and individuals' rights to privacy and to freedom from intimidation, harassment, and unwarranted annoyance. Appropriate use of computing and networking resources includes instruction; independent study; authorized research; independent research; communications; and official work of the offices, units, recognized student and campus organizations, and agencies of the University.

2.   DEFINITIONS

2.1.   Authorized use

Authorized use of Fort Valley State University-owned or operated computing and network resources is use consistent with the education, research, and service mission of the University, and consistent with this policy.

2.2.   Authorized users

Authorized users are: (1) current faculty, staff, and students of the University; (2) anyone connecting to a public information service (see section 6.5); (3) others whose access furthers the mission of the University and whose usage does not interfere with other users' access to resources. In addition, a user must be specifically authorized to use a network resource by the campus unit responsible for operating the resource.

3.   INDIVIDUAL PRIVILEGES

It is the following individual privileges, all of which are currently existent at Fort Valley State University, that empower each of us to be productive a member of the campus community. It must be understood that privileges are conditioned upon acceptance of the accompanying responsibilities.

3.1.   Privacy

To the greatest extent possible in a public setting we want to preserve the individual's privacy. Electronic and other technological methods must not be used to infringe upon privacy. However, users must recognize that Fort Valley State University computer systems and networks are public and subject to the Georgia Open Records Act. Users, thus, utilize such systems at their own risk.

3.2.   Freedom of expression

The constitutional right to freedom of speech applies to all members of the campus no matter the medium used.

3.3.   Ownership of intellectual works

People creating intellectual work using Fort Valley State University computers or networks, including but not limited to software, should consult related Fort Valley State University policies.

3.4.   Freedom from harassment and undesired information

All members of the campus have the right not to be harassed by computer or network usage by others. (See 4.1.3.)

4.   INDIVIDUAL RESPONSIBILITIES

Just as certain privileges are given to each member of the campus community, each of us is held accountable for our actions as a condition of continued membership in the community. The interplay of privileges and responsibilities within each individual situation and across campus engenders the trust and intellectual freedom that form the heart of our community. This trust and freedom are grounded on each person's developing the skills necessary to be an active and contributing member of the community. These skills include an awareness and knowledge about information and the technology used to process, store, and transmit it. Also, individuals are not allowed to assign, reassign or give others access to institutional resources (hardware, software and networks) without proper authorization.

4.1.   Common courtesy and respect for rights of others

You are responsible to all other members of the campus community in many ways, including to respect and value the rights of privacy for all, to recognize and respect the diversity of the population and opinion in the community, to behave ethically, and to comply with all legal restrictions regarding the use of information that is the property of others.

4.1.1.   Privacy of information

Files of personal information, including programs, no matter on what medium they are stored or transmitted, may be subject to the Georgia Open Records Act if stored on Fort Valley State University's computers. That fact notwithstanding, no one should look at, copy, alter, or destroy anyone else's personal files without explicit permission (unless authorized or required to do so by law or regulation). Simply being able to access file or other information does not imply permission to do so.

Similarly, no one should connect to a host on the network without advance permission in some form. People and organizations link computers to the network for numerous different reasons, and many consider unwelcome connects to be attempts to invade their privacy or compromise their security.

4.1.2. Intellectual property

You are responsible for recognizing (attributing) and honoring the intellectual property rights of others.

4.1.3. Harassment

No member of the community may, under any circumstances, use Fort Valley State University's computers or networks to libel, slander, or harass any other person.

The following shall constitute Computer Harassment: (1) Intentionally using the computer to annoy, harass, terrify, intimidate, threaten, offend or bother another person by conveying obscene language, pictures, or other materials or threats of bodily harm to the recipient or the recipient's immediate family; (2) Intentionally using the computer to contact another person repeatedly with the intent to annoy, harass, or bother, whether or not any actual message is communicated, and/or where no purpose of legitimate communication exists, and where the recipient has expressed a desire for the communication to cease; (3) Intentionally using the computer to contact another person repeatedly regarding a matter for which one does not have a legal right to communicate, once the recipient has provided reasonable notice that he or she desires such communication to cease (such as debt collection); (4) Intentionally using the computer to disrupt or damage the academic, research, administrative, or related pursuits of another; (5) Intentionally using the computer to invade the privacy, academic or otherwise, of another or the threatened invasion of the privacy of another.

4.2. Responsible use of resources

You are responsible for knowing what information resources (including networks) are available, remembering that the members of the community share them, and refraining from all acts that waste or prevent others from using these resources or from using them in whatever ways have been proscribed by the University and the laws of the State and Federal governments.

4.3. Game playing

Limited recreational game playing, that is not part of an authorized and assigned research or instructional activity, is tolerated (within the parameters of each department's rules). University computing and network services are not to be used for extensive or competitive recreational game playing. Recreational game players occupying a seat in a public computing facility must give up that seat when others who need to use the facility for academic or research purposes are waiting.

4.4. Information integrity

It is your responsibility to be aware of the potential for and possible effects of manipulating information, especially in electronic form, to understand the changeable nature of electronically stored information, and to verify the integrity and completeness of information that you compile or use. Do not depend on information or communications to be correct when they appear contrary to your expectations; verify it with the person who you believe originated the message or data.

4.5. Use of desktop systems

You are responsible for the security and integrity of University information stored on your personal desktop system. This responsibility includes making regular disk backups, controlling physical and network access to the machine, and installing and using virus protection software. Avoid storing passwords or other information that can be used to gain access to other campus computing resources.

4.6. Access to facilities and information

4.6.1. Sharing of access

Computer accounts, passwords, and other types of authorization are assigned to individual users and must not be shared with others. You are responsible for any use of your account.

4.6.2. Permitting unauthorized access

You may not run or otherwise configure software or hardware to intentionally allow access by unauthorized users. (See section 2.2.)

4.6.3. Use of privileged access

Special access to information or other special computing privileges are to be used in performance of official duties only. Information that you obtain through special privileges is to be treated as private.

4.6.4. Termination of access

When you cease being a member of the campus community (graduate or terminate employment), or if you are assigned a new position and/or responsibilities within the University, your access authorization must be reviewed. You must not use facilities, accounts, access codes, privileges, or information for which you are not authorized in your new circumstances.

4.7. Attempts to circumvent security

Users are prohibited from attempting to circumvent or subvert any system's security measures. This section does not prohibit use of security tools by system administration personnel.

4.7.1. Decoding access control information

You are prohibited from using any computer program or device to intercept or decode passwords or similar access control information.

4.7.2. Denial of service

Deliberate attempts to degrade the performance of a computer system or network or to deprive authorized personnel of resources or access to any University computer system or network are prohibited.

4.7.3. Harmful activities

The following harmful activities are prohibited: creating or propagating viruses; disrupting services; damaging files; intentional destruction of or damage to equipment, software, or data belonging to Fort Valley State University or other users; and the like.

4.7.4. Unauthorized access

You may not damage computer systems, obtain extra resources not authorized to you, deprive another user of authorized resources, gain unauthorized access to systems by using knowledge of a special password, loopholes in computer security systems, another user's password access abilities you used during a previous position at the University

4.7.5. Unauthorized monitoring

You may not use computing resources for unauthorized monitoring of electronic communications.

4.8. Academic dishonesty

You should always use computing resources in accordance with the high ethical standards of the University community. Academic dishonesty (plagiarism, cheating) is a violation of those standards.

4.9. Use of copyrighted information and materials

You are prohibited from using, inspecting, copying, and storing copyrighted computer programs and other material, in violation of copyright.

4.10. Use of licensed software

No software may be installed, copied, or used on University resources except as permitted by the owner of the software. Software subject to licensing must be properly licensed and all license provisions (installation, use, copying, number of simultaneous users, term of license, etc.) must be strictly adhered to.

4.11. Political campaigning; commercial advertising

Board of Regents policy (section 914.01) and the Fort Valley State University Faculty Handbook section (6.2.B.2) state "The use of System materials, supplies, equipment, machinery, or vehicles in political campaigns is forbidden." The use of University computers and networks shall conform to these policies.

4.12. Personal business

Computing facilities, services, and networks may not be used in connection with compensated outside work nor for the benefit of organizations not related to Fort Valley State University, except: in connection with scholarly pursuits (such as faculty publishing activities). This and any other incidental use (such as electronic communications or storing data on single-user machines) must not interfere with other users' access to resources (computer cycles, network bandwidth, disk space, printers, etc.) and must not be excessive. State law restricts the use of State facilities for personal gain or benefit.

5.   Fort Valley State University PRIVILEGES

Our society depends on institutions like Fort Valley State University to educate our citizens and advance the development of knowledge. However, in order to survive, Fort Valley State University must attract and responsibly manage financial and human resources. Therefore, Fort Valley State University has been granted by the State, and the various other institutions with which it deals, certain privileges regarding the information necessary to accomplish its goals and to the equipment and physical assets used in its mission.

5.1   Allocation of resources

Fort Valley State University may allocate resources in differential ways in order to achieve its overall mission.

5.2.   Control of access to information

Fort Valley State University may control access to its information and the devices on which it is stored, manipulated, and transmitted, in accordance with the laws of Georgia and the United States and the policies of the University and the Board of Regents.

5.3.   Imposition of sanctions

Fort Valley State University may impose sanctions and punishments on anyone who violates the policies of the University regarding computer and network usage.

5.4.   System administration access

System Administrator(s) (i.e., the person(s) responsible for the technical operations of a particular machine) may access others files for the maintenance of networks and computer and storage systems, such as to create backup copies of media. However, in all cases, all individuals, privileges and rights of privacy are to be preserved to the greatest extent possible.

5.5.   Monitoring of usage, inspection of files

Units of Fort Valley State University operating computers and networks may routinely monitor and log usage data, such as network session connection times and end-points, CPU and disk utilization for each user, security audit trails, network loading, etc. These units may review this data for evidence of violation of law or policy, and other purposes. When necessary, these units may monitor all the activities of and inspect the files of specific users on their computers and networks. Any person who believes such monitoring or inspecting is necessary must obtain the concurrence of the unit head and the ARPEC Committee. In all cases all individuals' privileges and right of privacy are to be preserved to the greatest extent possible.

5.6.   Suspension of individual privileges

Units of Fort Valley State University operating computers and networks may suspend computer and network privileges of an individual for reasons relating to his/her physical or emotional safety and well being, or for reasons relating to the safety and well-being of other members of the campus community, or University property. Access will be promptly restored when safety and well-being can be reasonably assured, unless access is to remain suspended as a result of formal disciplinary action imposed by the Office of the Vice President for Student Services (for students) or the employee's department in consultation with the office of Personnel Services (for employees).

6.   Fort Valley State University RESPONSIBILITIES

6.1.   Security procedures

Fort Valley State University has the responsibility to develop, implement, maintain, and enforce appropriate security procedures to ensure the integrity of individual and institutional information, however stored, and to impose appropriate penalties when privacy is purposefully abridged.

6.2.   Anti-harassment procedures

Fort Valley State University has the responsibility to develop, implement, maintain, and enforce appropriate procedures to discourage harassment by use of its computers or networks and to impose appropriate penalties when such harassment takes place.

6.3.   Upholding of copyrights and license provisions

Fort Valley State University has the responsibility to uphold all copyrights, laws governing access and use of information, and rules of organizations supplying information resources to members of the community (e.g., acceptable use policies for use of Internet).

6.4.   Individual unit responsibilities

Each unit has the responsibility of enforcing this policy providing for security in their areas, providing individuals equipped with University-owned desktop systems with resources for regular disk backups (software, hardware, media, and training) and for virus protection

If warranted by the importance and sensitivity of information stored and processed in their facility, a unit must also provide system administration personnel, perform and verify integrity of regular media backups, employ appropriate security-related software and procedures, guard confidentiality of private information, including user files and system access codes, control physical access to equipment, provide proper physical environment for equipment, provide safeguards against fire, flood, theft, etc., provide proper access administration; e.g., prompt and appropriate adjustment of access permissions upon a user's termination or transfer, control and record system software and configuration changes, monitor system logs for access control violation attempts

6.5.   Public information services

Units and individuals may, with the permission of the appropriate unit head, configure computing systems to provide information retrieval services to the public at large. (Current examples include "anonymous ftp" and "gopher.") However, in so doing, particular attention must be paid to the following sections of this policy: 2.1 (authorized use [must be consistent with University mission]), 3.3 (ownership of intellectual works), 4.2 (responsible use of resources), 4.9 (use of copyrighted information and materials), 4.10 (use of licensed software), and 6.4 (individual unit responsibilities). Usage of public services must not cause computer or network loading that impairs other services.

7.   PROCEDURES AND SANCTIONS

7.1.   Investigative contact

If you are contacted by a representative from an external organization (District Attorney's Office, FBI, GBI, Southern Bell Security Services, etc.) who is conducting an investigation of an alleged violation involving Fort Valley State University computing and networking resources, inform the office of Institution Research, Planning and Services (IRPS) immediately. Refer the requesting agency to the IRPS office; that office will provide guidance regarding the appropriate actions to be taken.

7.2.   Responding to security and abuse incidents

All users and units have the responsibility to report any discovered unauthorized access attempts or other improper usage of Fort Valley State University computers, networks, or other information processing equipment. If you observe, or have reported to you (other than as in 7.1 above), a security or abuse problem with any University computer or network facilities, including violations of this policy take immediate steps as necessary to ensure the safety and well-being of information resources. For example, if warranted, a system administrator should be contacted to temporarily disable any offending or apparently compromised computer accounts, or to temporarily disconnect or block offending computers from the network (see section 5.6).

Ensure that the following people are notified: (1)System Administrators, (2) your unit head.

The ARPEC will coordinate the technical and administrative response to such incidents. Reports of all incidents will be forwarded to Student Services (for apparent policy violations by students) or the unit head (for employees), and to the Director of IRPS and the Director of Computing & Information Technology Services.

7.3.   First and minor incident

If a person appears to have violated this policy, and (1) the violation is deemed minor by ARPEC, and (2) the person has not been implicated in prior incidents, then the incident may be dealt with at the ARPEC or unit level. The alleged offender will be furnished a copy of the University Computer and Network Usage Policy (this document), and will sign a form agreeing to conform to the policy.

7.4.   Subsequent and/or major violations

Reports of subsequent or major violations will be forwarded to Student Services (for students) or the unit head (for employees) for the determination of sanctions to be imposed. Units should consult the Office of Personnel Services regarding appropriate action.

7.5. Range of disciplinary sanctions

Persons in violation of this policy are subject to the full range of sanctions, including the loss of computer or network access privileges, disciplinary action, dismissal from the University, and legal action. Some violations may constitute criminal offenses, as outlined in the Georgia Computer Systems Protection Act and other local, state, and federal laws; the University will carry out its responsibility to report such violations to the appropriate authorities.

7.6. Appeals

Appeals should be directed through the already-existing procedure established for employees and students.

8. COMPUTING SUPPORT AND SERVICES

8.1 Definition of services and support

Services and support will be defined as those activities, relating to computers, both software and hardware, networking and data storage and retrieval, necessary to carry out job functions efficiently.

8.2 Requests for support and services

All departments/units must first request computing support and services from the Department of Computing and Information Technology Services.

8.3 Alternative services approval

All departments/units seeking services that cannot be provided by the Department of Computing and Information Technology Services must Receive approval from CITS.

8.4 Alternative services approval appeal

All request for alternative services denied by CITS may be appealed to ARPEC.

8.5 Approved alternative services

All alternative services negotiations pertaining to hardware, software, networking, maintenance (backups, upgrades and problem resolutions) and documentation must include the Director of CITS.

8.6 Approved alternative services specifications

Specifications for hardware, software, maintenance and networking requirements must be received in writing by the department/unit requesting the alternative services and reviewed and approved by the office of CITS before entering into any agreements with parties outside the University.

8.7 Final payment for services

Complete documentation, both user and system, must be received in writing before issuing final payment for services.

Computer Lab Policy

1. Overview

This document details the Acceptable Use and Ethics Policy which covers the proper utilization of the computers, networks and related services at Jacksonville State University. This policy has been developed to ensure a quality computing environment at JSU that furthers the academic, research and service mission of the **University**. Providing this environment requires equitable resource distribution, computer and network availability, personal privacy and data integrity. Achieving this goal requires that everyone in the **University** community cooperate and adhere to these guidelines.

2. Authorized Users

Individuals who have been granted and hold an active and authorized account on a JSU computer or network and abide by this policy are considered authorized users. Currently enrolled students who use JSU computer resources but do not have an account are also considered authorized users. Students using Academic Computer Services labs may be asked at any time to furnish proper student identification and may be asked to leave until proof of enrollment is given.

3. Authorized Use

Authorized use is that which is consistent with the academic, research and service goals of this institution and falls within the guidelines of this policy and the JSU Manual of Policies and Procedures.

4. Individual Rights

A. Privacy

The computing professionals at JSU are committed to preserving the privacy of each authorized user of the computer systems and make every effort to ensure that computers and electronic devices are not used to prevent this. However, it is impossible to guarantee such privacy and there are several specific issues that users must be aware of. Electronic mail messages are not secure and, therefore, should not be assumed to be private. Also, despite best efforts to prevent it, a determined person could gain unauthorized access to stored data and thus violate privacy. Finally, in the process of performing normal systems/network management and auditing functions, it may be necessary to view users' files or confidential information. However, system, network and application administrators are bound by both professional ethics as well as job requirements to respect the privacy of those involved and not initiate disclosure of information obtained in this manner.

B. Safety and Freedom from Harassment

While JSU cannot control harassment or unsolicited contact on the network, those who believe they have been harassed should report such violations to the proper authorities.

C. Access to Information

JSU does not guarantee users access to any site on the Internet nor is there any guarantee that access will be denied to any site. Users should be aware that there are services available on the Internet which may be considered offensive to some.

5. Individual Responsibilities

Users of JSU computer equipment are expected to understand this policy and abide by it. Questions regarding this policy can be directed to Academic Computer Services, Room 305 Bibb Graves Hall.

A. Morals and Ethics

Users are expected to respect the right to privacy of other individuals on the network. Accessing files of others is prohibited even if security permissions permit. It is expected that explicit permission from the owner of the files is obtained before they are accessed.

B. Expected Behaviors

This section details some guidelines relating to computer based activities. JSU computer users are expected to read signon messages and system news for specific information such as system changes, policies and scheduled downtime. Additionally, valuable information is available in the JSU World Wide Web pages and the various JSU newsgroups related to computing. System and network administrators may find it necessary to contact computer users regarding policy issues. If repeated attempts to contact an individual are unsuccessful, the system or network administrator may be forced to temporarily deactivate the account simply to compel the owner to make return contact.

C. Userids and Passwords

It is a violation of policy to use a computer userid (or any computer resource) assigned to another user or to share a userid or password with other individuals (including computing personnel). A computer userid is granted to an individual and that individual is responsible for any use of the account. If a user knowingly shares a password with someone else and this policy is violated, the user will also be subject to the sanctions outlined in Section 6.0. If file sharing with others is necessary, there are methods and techniques to accomplish this without sharing userids and passwords. Users should follow guidelines for password selection which include choosing a password that cannot be easily guessed by others, changing it often, and verifying the last login time. Remember that the password is the first line of defense against unauthorized access to an account.

D. Providing Services

Users are not permitted to provide network or computer-based services using JSU computers or networks without prior permission from the department responsible for the computers or networks in question. Examples of such services include, but are not limited to, FTP, WEB, and GOPHER servers.

E. Unauthorized Access

A user must not attempt to guess or break another user's password. Any attempt to gain unauthorized access to JSU computers and networks is prohibited. Users may not use JSU facilities to login or attempt to login to computers external to JSU to which they are not authorized. Anyone suspecting that their account has been compromised should contact Academic Computer Services or the department responsible for issuing the account.

F. Unauthorized Monitoring

Users are not permitted to use computers and networks to monitor or attempt to monitor electronic transmissions.

G. Disruption of Service

Deliberate attempts to disrupt the operation or degrade the performance of computers or networks are prohibited.

H. Disruption of Resources

Users are prohibited from circumventing or attempting to circumvent any policies or procedures that have been established to ensure equitable resource distribution in the JSU shared computing environment. (For example, leaving a book beside a computer in a lab for an extended period of time to keep others from using the system.)

I. Mass Electronic Mailings

University-wide electronic mailings are not permitted without prior permission due to the heavy use of resources this requires. In general, there are better and more efficient ways to make information globally available. Use of the JSU newsgroups is encouraged for these activities.

J. Game Playing and Recreational Activities

The policy regarding game playing on JSU computers and networks is established by the department responsible for the computers and networks in question. Game playing and other recreational activities which do not contribute to completion of JSU academic requirements are prohibited in Academic Computer Services labs. No department should permit game playing to interfere with normal **University** business.

K. Business Use

Use of JSU computers or networks for non-JSU business purposes or non-JSU related employment is prohibited.

L. Use of Copyrighted or Licensed Materials

There shall be no copying or installation of software on JSU computers if such copying or installation would violate any copyright or licensing agreement. Users may be asked to show a valid license agreement to ensure the legal use of software on JSU computers. Contact the department head or lab supervisor responsible for the specific computer for any questions regarding licensing issues.

M. JSU News Groups

Users must abide by the established rules of conduct of Usenet, also known as "netiquette".

6. Sanctions

Violators of this policy may be subject to one or more of the following sanctions which can be imposed by the department responsible for the computers and networks on which the violation occurred:

1. Admonition

2. Temporary or permanent suspension of computer privileges

3. Temporary or permanent suspension of lab privileges

Additional sanctions may also apply as outlined in the JSU Student Handbook.

A. Legal Restraints

Users of JSU computing facilities are expected to abide by State and Federal laws that apply to the usage of computers. Any violation of these laws will be reported to the proper authorities.

B. Appeals

Appeals to sanctions should be handled through the existing **University** grievance and appeals policy.

Section XXV

To Library Policy Manual Table of Contents

To Electronic Reference Desk Page

To Library Home Page

To JSU Homepage

Last Update: November 1, 2001
Suggestions or Comments contact: Doug Taylor or Jodi Poe

Item: Messiah College Computing Access Policy

Last Revision: 09/15/98

Purpose: Messiah College seeks to provide a user friendly computing environment that supports the goals and mission of the college.

POLICY

The Computing Access policy applies to anyone who uses the college's computers and networks, and articulates the standards of behavior that are expected of all users. The Director of Information Technology Services is responsible to administer this policy, and to make referrals to appropriate administrative offices for any disciplinary action. Any exception to this policy must be approved in writing by the Director of Information Technology Services.

A. General Guidelines. The college reserves the right to regulate any activity that occurs on the campus network or on any other computer based system owned by the college. This includes, but is not limited to, the following implications:
1. Anyone who uses the campus computing environment must have appropriate status (staff, faculty, current students, etc.) and must be properly authorized when required.
2. Anyone not adhering to college policy should expect any or all of the following disciplinary actions:
a. Restriction or suspension of access privileges.
b. Referral to the appropriate disciplinary authority of the college.
c. Referral to the appropriate local, state or federal authority for legal prosecution.
3. Material (software, hardware or data) that is found to be in violation of this policy can be banned, confiscated, or otherwise eliminated from the college computing environment.
4. The college will be as pro-active as possible to ensure compliance with this policy, including surveillance commensurate with appropriate maintenance of the right to privacy.

B. Restrictions. Users must not engage in activity outside the limits of access that have been authorized for them. This includes but is not limited to:
1. Performing an act that negatively impacts the operation of computers, peripherals or networks, or that impedes the ability of someone else to do his/her work. Examples include but are not limited to:
a. Tampering with any transmission medium or hardware device, or connecting any unauthorized device or computer to the college network.
b. Propagating a software virus or worm.
c. Damaging or destroying data owned by the college or someone else.
d. Modifying any disk or software directory provided by the college for any type of special use.
e. Performing an act that places an unnecessary load on a shared computer or the college network. A specific example would be to play a network based computer game that significantly degrades the performance of the college network.
2. Attempting to circumvent protection schemes for access to data or systems, or otherwise uncover security loopholes.
3. Gaining or granting unauthorized access to computers, devices, software or data. This includes, but is not limited to:
a. Admitting someone into a locked facility, such as a computer lab, or unlocking any facility that is normally locked, without permission.
b. Revealing a password to any account, including one's own personal account, without permission.
c. Permitting the use of any account, including one's own personal account, in a way that allows unauthorized access to resources.
4. Using the college's facilities to broadcast unauthorized personal messages to large segments of the user community. Examples include but are not limited to:
a. Advertising campaigns for personal financial gain or political purposes.
b. Pranks and chain messages.
c. Announcements not approved for dissemination by this method.

C. Expectations. Users must abide by all applicable laws or government regulations, and operate within the limits articulated by the college for ethical and moral behavior. Examples include but are not limited to:

1. Using any material in violation of any software licensing agreement or copyright law.
2. Using software or data that infringes on the rights of others. Specific examples include the production or propagation of material that is abusive, profane or sexually, racially or religiously offensive; or material that may injure or harass someone else, or lead to a lawsuit or criminal charges.
3. Using college equipment or infrastructure to access off-campus resources (including materials on the Internet) in a manner that is in violation of the ethical or moral standards of the college. A specific example would be to obtain inappropriate material from the World Wide Web using a computer in one of the college's computer labs.
4. Using personal equipment connected to the college infrastructure to access off-campus resources (including materials on the Internet) in a manner that is in violation of the ethical or moral standards of the college. A specific example would be to obtain inappropriate material from the World Wide Web using a personally owned computer connected to the Internet via a college network connection in a residence hall room.
5. Monitoring someone else's data communications, or otherwise reading, copying, changing or deleting files or software without proper permission of the owner.
6. Using college facilities for personal gain, or for the benefit of an organization other than the college, without permission.

D. Social Responsibility. This policy further calls on everyone who is part of the college community to recognize the need for social responsibility. This includes but is not limited to the following implications:

1. Being good stewards of the environment. Examples include but are not limited to:
   a. Using but not abusing the equipment provided, i.e. helping to make equipment last as long as possible.
   b. Being conservative in the use of supplies, such as paper provided for printing.
2. Being respectful of others, remembering:
   a. Your work is not necessarily more important than someone else's.
   b. There are rules for the use of each lab that can vary from lab to lab. Be sensitive to someone who's work may have a higher priority than yours for the specific lab being used.
3. Confronting one another in love when necessary. Students should be talking with each other, and as situations dictate, should report problems to college personnel. Examples include:
   a. Accessing material on the Internet that is inappropriate.
   b. Ignoring usage guidelines for a particular lab.
   c. Behaving in ways that could damage and/or disrupt access to college computing resources.

E. College Policies. Users of the college computing environment must abide by all other applicable Messiah College policies. Examples include but are not limited to:

1. The software piracy policy.
2. Usage authorization requirements and procedures.
3. Usage restrictions, physical access regulations, and behavioral expectations established for each location containing equipment designated for public use. Examples: games policy, location specific software usage priorities, etc.
4. Usage requirements and restrictions for network connections in residence hall rooms.

Mount Union College

Computing Ethics Policy

Standards of Conduct

The general standards of conduct expected of members of the Mount Union College community also apply to the use of the College computers, network facilities, information services and resources. These facilities and resources include: wiring or infrastructure used for communications; electronics, digital switches and communication equipment used for processing or communications; programs, programming languages, instructions, or routines which are used to perform work on a computer; digital information such as records, images, sounds, video or textual material stored on or accessible through a computer; computers used for automation or the administration of information services; information such as I.D.s, authorization codes, account numbers, usage and billing records, or textual material stored on or accessible through the network or other communication lines.

Property Rights

College computers, network facilities, information services and resources are made available to individuals to assist in the pursuit of educational goals. In order to promote the most effective use of these, it is expected that users will cooperate with each other and respect the privacy of information even though it may be in electronic form rather than printed form. Individuals and organizations will be held no less accountable for their actions in situations involving College computers, network facilities, information services and resources than they would be in dealing with other media. Though some of them are intangible, these College computers, network facilities, information services and resources are the property of the College. Rules prohibiting theft or vandalism apply to authorization codes, long distance telephone services, television signals and service information as well as to physical equipment. Conduct which violates the College's property rights with respect to College computers, network facilities, information services and resources is subject to College disciplinary action. This conduct includes: using College computers, network facilities, information services and resources for purposes other than those intended by the College body granting access to those resources (especially using them for personal financial gain or allowing access to them by unauthorized persons even if they are members of the College community); using any portion of College computers, network facilities, information services and resources for the purpose of copying College-owned or licensed information to another computer system for personal or external use without prior written approval, attempting to modify College-owned or licensed information (including software and data) without prior approval, or attempting to damage or disrupt the operation of computer equipment, communications equipment, or communications lines; knowingly accepting or using College-owned or licensed information (including software and data) which has been obtained by illegal means; from a single faceplate, receiving more than one set of television signals or distributing these signals to multiple receivers; or knowingly accepting or using television signals which have been obtained by illegal means.

Confidentiality

The College seeks to protect the civil, personal, and property rights of those actually using its computers, network facilities, information services and resources and seeks to protect the confidentiality of College records stored on its computer systems. The College also seeks similarly to protect those computers, network facilities, information services and resources of other institutions to whom College personnel have access via the College computers, network facilities, information services and resources. Conduct which involves the use of College computers, network facilities, information services and resources to violate another's rights is subject to College disciplinary action. This conduct includes: invading the privacy of an individual by using electronic means to ascertain confidential information, even if an individual or department inadvertently allows access to information; copying another user's information without the permission of the owner, even if it is readily accessible by electronic means; knowingly accepting or using information which has been obtained by illegal means; or abusing or harassing another user using the College computers, network facilities, information services and resources.

Accessibility/Use

Some of the College computers, network facilities, information services and resources require that each user have a unique identity (i.e., User-name). The identity is used to represent a user in various College computers, network facilities, information services and resources based on his/her credibility and purpose for requiring such access; and to associate his/her own service use and information with his/her identity. As such, this identity is another instrument of identification and its misuse constitutes forgery or misrepresentation. Conduct which involves inappropriate access or misuse of College computers, network facilities, information services or resources and service identities is subject to College disciplinary action. This conduct includes: allowing another individual to use ones unique identity; using another individual's identity, even if the individual has neglected to safeguard it; using the College computers, network facilities, information services and resources in the commission of a crime; gaining access to non-public computers, network facilities, information services and resources. Mount Union College's computers, network facilities, information services and resources are networked on the Mount Union College campus and to other locations. Information on the College's networks and communication lines is considered to be private. Tapping the College's network or communication lines for the purpose of examining or using information other than that destined for the intended user is considered unacceptable conduct and is subject to disciplinary action.

Disciplinary Actions

Violators will be subject to the usual judicial procedures of the College; the loss of computing privileges and/or employment may result. Abuse of the networks or of computers at other sites connected to the networks will be treated as abuse of computing privileges at Mount Union College. Conduct in violation of the principles set forth above, with respect to the use of College information services and facilities, may also be subject to criminal or civil legal action in addition to College disciplinary action. It should be understood that this policy does not preclude enforcement under the laws and regulations of the State of Ohio and/or the United States of America. Any questions concerning ethical or legal use of computing facilities should be directed to the Director of Computer Information Services.

Last updated: *February 25, 1998*
Please send comments and suggestions to *helpdesk@muc.edu*

Acceptable Use Policies

This policy gives a general outline of the expectations of all those using Reed College's computers.

Reed College computer equipment is provided for use by all Reed students, faculty and staff. Alumni and, other individuals may, in some cases, use computer facilities as guests of the College. All eligible individuals who wish to use the computer facilities are required to endorse a user agreement and are expected to follow the guidelines for acceptable computer use which are described below.

Acceptable Uses

Reed's computer facilities are provided for academic and educational purposes only. Examples of acceptable uses are:

- Coursework and course management

- Thesis preparation

- Independent research and self-teaching projects

- Communication with students and faculty at other academic or research institutions

Prohibited Uses

In general, any uses of Reed's computer facilities which (1) infringe on another individual's right to privacy, (2) adversely affect the user community, (3) are not allowed under the terms of our software licenses, or (4) are illegal, are prohibited. Examples of prohibited uses are:

- Unauthorized reading, copying, or modification of someone else's files or electronic mail, unauthorized use of someone else's password, or distribution of your password

- Intentional damage to hardware, software, security devices or codes or the intentional creation or distribution of viruses, worms or other forms of electronic mayhem

- Unauthorized Internet access to computers at other locations

- Abuse of printing privileges, such as printing multiple copies or printing under a false user name

- Sending obscene or abusive messages

- Commercial activities, such as development of software for sale, work undertaken to support any company, or contract work unrelated to Reed's academic mission

- Excessive non-academic use of network bandwidth

- Excessive non-academic use of server CPU

- Persistent and unattended use of non-academic software (e.g. IRC 'bots)

- Unauthorized duplication of commercial software or other copyrighted material, such as music, images, text or multimedia.

Illegal Copying of Software and Other Copyrighted Materials

Respect for intellectual labor and creativity is vital to academic discourse and enterprise. This principle applies to works of all authors and publishers in all media. It encompasses respect for the right to acknowledgment, right to privacy, and right to determine the form, manner, and terms of publication and distribution of one's work. Because electronic information is volatile and easily reproduced, respect for the work and personal expression of others is especially critical in computer environments. Violations of authorship integrity, including plagiarism, invasion of privacy, unauthorized access, and trade secret and copyright violations, may be grounds for sanctions against members of the academic community. It is illegal to make unauthorized copies of software or other copyrighted material. Copyright laws protect authors and publishers of software, music, images, and multimedia materials, just as they protect authors of printed materials.

Reed College

Widespread use of illegally copied software or other materials undermines Reed's ability to negotiate favorable software agreements and may result in legal action against the College. Reed does not condone the use of illegally copied software and will not provide assistance and support to users of such software.

⬤ Failure to Comply

Failure to comply with guidelines for acceptable use of computer resources may cause the user to be denied access to College computing equipment.

CUS reserves the right to deny an account to anyone who has violated the user agreement, or fails to pay required fees for printing, network connections, or accounts as described above. The terms and conditions for usage are subject to change as computing resources and user demands vary. This usage policy will be reviewed on a regular basis and users will be notified of any changes.

For further information, contact the Reed College Office of Computer User Services at 503-777-7525 or via electronic mail at cus@reed.edu.

Last modified: October 26, 2000

State University of New York at Geneseo

Computing and Network Access Policies

Access to modern information technology is essential to the State University of New York mission of providing the students, faculty and staff of SUNY Geneseo with educational services of the highest quality. The pursuit and achievement of the SUNY mission of education, research, and public service require that the privilege of the use of computing systems and software, internal and external data networks, as well as access to the World Wide Web, be made available to all those of the SUNY Geneseo community. The preservation of that privilege for the full community requires that each faculty member, staff member, student, and other authorized user comply with institutional and external standards for appropriate use.

To assist and ensure such compliance, SUNY Geneseo establishes the following policy which supplements all applicable SUNY policies, including sexual harassment, patent and copyright, and student and employee disciplinary policies, as well as applicable federal and state laws. *

1. Authorized Use

SUNY Geneseo computer facilities are a resource for members of the campus community, to be utilized for work consistent with the instructional, research, and administrative goals of the College.

As a condition for use of the computing facilities, all users must adhere to the regulations below.

A. Authorized Activities

SUNY Geneseo computer facilities and network shall be utilized solely for work consistent with the instructional, research, and administrative goals of the College, as defined in the SUNY Geneseo "Missions and Goals" statement and the SUNY Policy Manual, Item 007.1. Geneseo computer facilities and network may not be used to post or transmit any material that constitutes or contains advertising or any solicitation of product or services in exchange for personal financial gain.

B. User Privacy

Users shall respect the privacy of others. Users shall not intentionally view information of other users, modify or obtain copies of other users' files, or modify other users' passwords without their permission. Geneseo computers and networks are designed to protect user privacy; users shall not attempt to circumvent these protections. Unauthorized "port scanning", the scanning of network services on local or remote computers, is expressly forbidden.

C. System Integrity

Users shall respect the system integrity of campus computing facilities. For example, users shall not intentionally develop or use programs that infiltrate a computing system, or damage or alter the software components of a computing or network system. Authorized personnel routinely monitor the network and occasionally will require access to state owned equipment on the network.

D. Resource Accounting

Users shall not develop or use procedures to alter or avoid the accounting and monitoring of the use of computing facilities. For example, users may not utilize facilities anonymously or by means of an alias, and may not send messages, mail, or print files that do not show the correct username of the user performing the operation.

E. Resource Contention & Efficient Use

Users shall use the computing facilities in a responsible and efficient manner. They are expected to refrain from deliberately wasteful practices such as printing unnecessary listings, performing endless unnecessary computations, or unnecessarily holding public computers or dial-up phone lines for long periods of time when others are waiting for the same resources. Users shall not develop or use procedures that obstruct authorized use by others. Users shall not interfere with microcomputer setups, such as PCRDist and RevRDist, which are intended to keep microcomputer software current and legal. Users shall not use applications that use an unusually high portion of the network bandwidth for extended periods of time, thus inhibiting the use of the network by others. Users shall avoid wasting computing resources by excessive game playing or other trivial applications; by sending chain letters or other frivolous or excessive messages locally or over the network.

F. Copyrights and Licenses

Users shall not violate the legal protection provided by copyrights and licenses held by SUNY Geneseo. Users shall not make copies of any licensed or copyrighted computer program found on any SUNY Geneseo computer or storage device without the written authorization of Computing & Information Technology. US Federal copyright law grants authors certain exclusive rights of reproduction, adaptation, distribution, performance, display, attribution, and integrity to their creations. Works of literature, photographs, music, software, film, and video works can all be copyrighted. Examples of probable violations of copyright laws include, but are not limited to: making unauthorized copies of any copyrighted material (such as commercial software, text, graphic images, audio, and video recordings), or distributing copyrighted materials over computer networks or through other means.

G. Residential Network

Users shall not use the residential network to provide Internet access to anyone outside of the College community for any purpose other than those that are in direct support of the academic mission of the College. A computer user must not encroach on other users' access and use of the College's computing and networking resources. Examples include: excessive use of bandwidth; sending chain letters or extensive messages, either locally or off-campus; unauthorized modification of system facilities; and attempts to disable or tie-up a computer or network. Network services and wiring may not be tampered with or extended beyond the area of their intended use. This applies to all network wiring, hardware and in-room jacks.

H. Personal Web Pages

Users are encouraged to create their own web pages. Faculty, staff and students have access to a personal directory on the College server where they can maintain their own web page files. Under no circumstances should personal space and/or files be shared with other users. In designing a personal home page, keep in mind that home pages may not be used for personal profit, contain pornography or obscene material, violate copyright or any other state or federal laws. Personal home pages will not be screened. However, the College reserves the right to monitor all pages on the server and respond to complaints about a web page. The College may remove files if it feels that computing policies have been violated. In addition, failure to comply with computing policies could, in some cases, lead to disciplinary action or criminal prosecution.

I. Recreational/Personal Use

Recreational use of computing facilities, including computer games and social network communication, is allowed only when no other instructional, research, or administrative function requires the resources being used. Anyone using a computer for recreational purposes is required to relinquish the computer immediately to someone needing it for academic or administrative purposes. For faculty and staff, personal use of computers and the Internet is not prohibited but should not negatively affect the timely completion of work.

J. Academic Dishonesty

Practicing any form of dishonesty through use of computing facilities (for example cheating, plagiarism, or fraud) is prohibited.

K. Harassment

Using computers or networks to harass, abuse or intimidate another person is prohibited. Users shall not develop or use programs that harass other users or render other computers inoperable. Users shall be sensitive to the public nature of the college, and take care not to display on screens in such locations images, sounds or messages that could create an atmosphere of discomfort or harassment for others.

L. Obscenity

Obscene language in electronic mail, messages, process names, file names, file data, web pages, and other publicly visible forms is prohibited. The definition of obscenity is found in Article 235 of New York State Penal Code.

M. Pornography

Federal Child Pornography Law makes it illegal to create, possess, or distribute graphic depiction of minors engaged in sexual activity, including computer graphics. Computers storing such information can be seized as evidence.

2. Authorization

Computing & Information Technology authorizes the use of SUNY Geneseo computer facilities by members of the campus community. All who use SUNY Geneseo computer facilities have the responsibility to do so in an effective, efficient, ethical, and legal manner, as outlined below.

A. User Accounts

Use of SUNY Geneseo's computer systems requires that a user account be issued by the College, granting access to a particular system. Every computer user account issued by SUNY Geneseo is the responsibility of the person in whose name it is issued. College recognized clubs and student organizations may be issued a user account. Faculty advisors shall designate a particular person(s) authorized to act on behalf of the club or organization. This person(s) is responsible for all activity on the account and will be subject to College disciplinary procedures for misuse. The following will be considered theft of services, and subject to penalties described in Section 3, below.

(1) Acquiring a username in another person's name;

(2) Using a username without the explicit permission of the owner and of Computing & Information Technology;

(3) Allowing one's username to be used by another person without explicit permission of Computing & Information Technology.

B. Restricted Access Systems

Access to selected administrative computers and programs is restricted on a "need-to-know" basis conforming to State University of New York policy guidelines. Unauthorized access or attempted access to these machines or data will constitute theft of services and will be subject to the penalties described in Section 3, below. Authorization for use of these systems is granted solely by Computing & Information Technology, and reviewed by the campus Security Administrator.

C. Password Security

It is mandatory that user accounts be kept secure by keeping passwords secret, and changing the passwords often. Users must set a password which will protect their account from unauthorized use, and which will not be guessed easily. Avoid selecting easily guessable passwords, for example nicknames and phone numbers. Users must report to Computing & Information Technology any use of a user account without the explicit permissions of the owner and of Computing & Information Technology.

D. Microcomputing

Use of SUNY Geneseo microcomputing facilities does not generally require that a user account be issued. The authorization to utilize College microcomputer facilities is granted to members of the campus community on condition that they adhere to the regulations specified in Authorized Use. While the public is not barred, Geneseo faculty, staff and students have priority use over microcomputing facilities. Public users may be asked to yield to Geneseo faculty, staff and students at any time. Microcomputing access may be granted to minors with written permission from your parent/guardian.

3. Violation of policy

Violation of the policy above is unethical and may constitute a criminal offense. Violations of this policy disrupt the computing environment at the College and will be dealt with according to the following sections.

A. Definition of an violation

Violations are defined by and will be dealt with according to any or all of the following: applicable Federal laws; Article 156 and Section 165.15 of the New York State Penal Law; the SUNY Geneseo "Student Code of Conduct"; other laws, regulations, and policies of the College, the State University of New York, the State of New York and the United States of America. Violations may result in the suspension or permanent closing of usernames, campus disciplinary action resulting in up to and including academic dismissal or termination of employment, legal action and/or other action.

B. Investigation of a violation

When Computing & Information Technology becomes aware of a possible violation, we will initiate an investigation in conjunction with the campus Security Administrator and/or relevant campus offices including the Dean of Students, Personnel Office, and University Police. Users are expected to cooperate fully in such investigations when requested.

In order to prevent further unauthorized activity during the course of such an investigation, Computing & Information Technology may suspend authorization for use of all computing facilities for the user(s) involved in the violation.

4. Definitions

*Throughout this document, the following definitions apply:

(1) Computing Facilities include all mainframes, minicomputers, personal computers, networks, Internet Service and computer peripherals owned or operated by SUNY Geneseo.

(2) Users are individuals who make use of SUNY Geneseo computing facilities. Most users are students, faculty, and staff members of SUNY Geneseo. Some users are non-campus personnel authorized by the campus to make use of computing facilities, including volunteers for local non-profit agencies, scholars visiting from other SUNY institutions, and the like.

(3) A Username is a unique code assigned to each large system user by the SUNY Geneseo Computing & Information Technology. When used with a password chosen by the user, the username allows access to the large system computing facilities of the College.

Tarleton State University

Computer Use Regulations

Approved 01/14/2001

Table of Contents

Introduction

Tarleton State University provides each of its students, faculty and staff with one or more computer accounts (user-Ids) that permit use of the University's technology resources. Use of these resources is a privilege, not a right. When using these resources, individuals agree to abide by the applicable rules, regulations, and policies of the University, as well as federal, state and local laws. The University reserves the right to limit, restrict or deny access to its technology resources, as well as to take disciplinary and/or legal action against anyone in violation of these regulations or applicable law.

Applicable Rules, Regulations, Policies, and Laws

Users of the University's technology resources must comply with the rules and regulations outlined in this document but must also comply with other University rules and regulations and with The Texas A&M University System (TAMUS) policies against harassment, plagiarism, and unethical conduct and any procedures that govern computer usage at a particular facility on campus.

Laws that apply to users of the University's technology resources include, but are not limited to, federal, state and local laws pertaining to theft, copyright infringement, insertion of viruses into computer systems, and other computer related crimes.

These regulations apply to all University technology resources, including but not limited to single-user microcomputers, multi-user servers and mainframes, and the network infrastructure, and includes resources administered centrally or within a department. Technology resources include hardware, software, communications networks, electronic storage media, and documentation. Data includes all files, regardless of size or storage media, including e-mail messages, system logs, and software (commercial or locally developed).

Principles

The following principles address the general philosophy of Tarleton State University on computer use and security. These principles apply to and are binding on all users of University technology resources:

Authorized Use: Tarleton State University provides technology resources for the purpose of accomplishing tasks related to the University's mission.

It should be noted that the use of some computers, networks, and software located on the University campus may be dedicated for specific research, teaching missions or purposes that limit their use or access.

Students who have paid their fees will be allowed to use the University's technology resources for school-related and personal purposes, subject to these regulations, other applicable policies, and state and federal law; and as long as personal use does not result in any additional costs to the University. Students who have graduated or who leave the University for any reason will have their computer accounts terminated. Continuing students enrolled for the spring semester who do not graduate may retain their computer account(s) during the summer.

An employee of the University shall be allowed to use technology resources in accordance with these regulations and other applicable policies. Incidental personal use of technology resources by employees is permitted, subject to review and reasonable restrictions by the employee's supervisor; adherence to applicable rules, regulations, and policies and state and federal law; and as long as such usage does not interfere with the employee's accomplishment of his or her job duties and does not result in any additional costs to the University. When an employee terminates employment, his or her access to the University's technology resources will be terminated immediately.

Privacy: Users of the University's computer systems should be aware that computer use may be subject to:

    1. Review or disclosure in accordance with the Texas Public Information Act and other laws;
    2. Administrative review of computer use for security purposes, for investigation of policy or legal compliance, or during computer system maintenance; and

3. Audit as required to protect the reasonable interests of the University and other users of the computer system.

In using the University's computer systems, users expressly consent to University monitoring for these purposes and is advised that if such monitoring reveals possible evidence of criminal activity, the University administration may provide that evidence to law enforcement officials. Further, all users should understand that the University is unable to guarantee the protection of electronic files, data or e-mails from unauthorized or inappropriate access.

Intellectual Property: All members of the University community should be aware that intellectual property laws extend to the electronic environment. Users should assume that works communicated through the computer network are subject to copyright laws, unless specifically stated otherwise.

Valuable assets: Technology resources and data are considered valuable assets of the University. Further, computer software purchased or leased by the University is the property of the University or the company from whom it is leased. Any unauthorized access, use, alteration, duplication, destruction, or disclosure of any of these technology resources may constitute a computer-related crime, punishable under Texas statutes and federal laws. University technology resources may not be transported without appropriate authorization.

Users Must:

1. **Know and obey the specific policies established for the systems and networks they access.**
2. **Comply with laws, policies, regulations, license agreements, and contracts that pertain to and limit the use of the University's technology resources.**
3. **Use the University technology resources responsibly, respecting the needs of other computer users.** All users must manage their email accounts to remain within the University stipulated disk quotas. Users should maintain the secrecy of their account name (s) and password(s).
4. **Report any observed or known misuse of technology resources or violations of these regulations to a computer lab supervisor, the help desk, a department head, or the Office of Information Resources.**
5. **Comply with all reasonable requests and instructions from the computer system operators/administrators.**
6. **Reflect high ethical standards, mutual respect and civility when communicating with others via the University computer system.**

a. Respect the rights of others to freedom from harassment or intimidation.

b. Be polite and courteous.
c. Use caution when giving out addresses or phone numbers (both yours and others).
d. Practice network etiquette when communicating electronically.

Users Must NOT:

1. **Commit illegal acts**. University technology resources are not to be used in support of or for illegal activities. Any such use will be reported and dealt with by the appropriate University authorities and/or law enforcement agencies. Illegal use may involve, but is not limited to, unauthorized access, intentional corruption or misuse of technology resources, theft, obscenity, and child pornography.

2. **Use the University computer system in a manner that violates other rules, regulations, and policies such as racial, ethnic, religious, sexual or other forms of harassment or intimidation.**

3. **Use the University's computer system for the transmission of commercial or personal advertisements, solicitations, promotions, or political material without approval obtained through University-established channels.**

   a. A bulletin board is currently provided for personal use.
   b. The appropriate vice president may grant approval for faculty and staff and the Dean of Student Life may grant approval for students.

4. **Use the distribution lists for faculty, staff and students to send information other than official University business.** A brief description of the guidelines for use of distribution lists is included in this document.

5. **Distribute copyrighted materials without providing written permission from the author to the University or determining that use of the materials complies with copyright laws.**

6. **Duplicate commercial software. All commercial software is covered by a license agreement or copyright of some form.**

7. **Misrepresent one's identity via electronic or any other form of communication.** Use of someone else's access information is prohibited.

8. **Abuse technology resources** including, but not limited to:

a. Endangering or damaging specific computer software, hardware, program, network or the system as a whole, whether located on campus or elsewhere on the global Internet;

b. Creating or purposefully allowing a computer malfunction or interruption of operation; i.e., injection of a computer virus on to the computer system;

c. Disrupting University operations or the operations of outside entities. Applications that use an unusually large portion of the bandwidth for extended periods of time and applications designed to send repeated email messages or mass email messages are not permitted;

d. Printing that ties up technology resources for an unreasonable time period; and

e. Failing to adhere to applicable time limits for particular computer facilities.

9. **Breach security systems.**

a. Failing to protect a password or account from unauthorized use.

b. Permitting someone to use another's computer account, or using someone else's computer account. (The Executive Director of Information Resources will develop procedures to govern any exceptions to this rule.)

c. Using, accessing, duplicating, disclosing, altering, damaging, or destroying data contained on any electronic file, program, network, or University hardware or software without authorization.

d. Accessing any systems, software, or data for which you are not authorized. Sharing access to copyrighted software or other copyrighted material on the network is prohibited. University specific network resources or network resources obtained commercially by the University may not be transmitted outside of the University community.

e. Attempting to circumvent, assisting someone else or requesting that someone else circumvent any security measure or administrative access control that pertains to University technology resources.

10. **Modify or extend the network wiring and/or services beyond the area of its intended use.** This applies to all network wiring, hardware, and in-room jacks.

a. Using hub/hublet is prohibited unless provided by Information Resources.

b. Providing Intranet or Internet access to anyone outside

of the University community for any purpose is prohibited. Under no circumstances may users give others access to the University systems.
c. Providing network services from user computers is prohibited. Users who have an academic need to provide such services from their personal computer must present a written request to Information Resources and be granted permission prior to activating any such services on the network.

11. **Use the name "Tarleton State University" in any form or use any symbol, logo, or graphic associated with Tarleton State University for any purpose.** An exception to these requirements is when engaged in duties authorized by your position as an employee of the University or, if a student, engaged in University sanctioned academic or extracurricular activities. See the Office of Publications and Graphic Design for questions concerning use of these items.

Sanctions for Failure to Adhere to these Regulations

Alleged violations of these regulations shall be processed according to the established procedures outlined in the Tarleton State University Faculty Handbook, the Staff Handbook and the Student Handbook. The University treats access and use violations of computing facilities, equipment, software, information resources, networks, or privileges seriously. Abuse may subject the offender to prosecution under appropriate laws. The Dean of Student Life will process student violations, and faculty and staff violations will be processed using the appropriate lines of authority.

It is important to note that failure to adhere to these regulations may lead to the cancellation of a user's computer account(s), suspension from the University, dismissal, or other disciplinary action by the University, as well as referral to legal and law enforcement agencies. A user's computer account(s) may be suspended temporarily until the violation has been processed or permanently at the discretion of the appropriate University official.

Responsibilities of Deans, Department Heads, and Supervisors

1. **Ensure that employees within a department comply with these regulations and other applicable University policies and are given reasonable opportunities to attend appropriate training.**
2. **Promptly inform the Office of Information Resources when employees have been terminated so that the terminated employee's access to University technology resources may be disabled.**
3. **Promptly report ongoing or serious problems regarding computer use to the Office of Information Resources.**

<u>Auditor Access of University Computing Resources</u>

There will be occasions when auditors require access to University technology resources and data files. The access will be permitted in accordance with these guidelines:

Internal Auditors from The Texas A&M University System:

o Shall be allowed access to all University activities, records, property, and employees in the performance of their duties.

State and Federal Auditors:

o State and Federal auditors will be granted access to University technology resources and data files on an as needed basis, as approved by the Office of Information Resources and the Office of General Counsel, The Texas A&M University System.

<u>Laws That Pertain To Computer Usage:</u>

Texas Administrative Code, 201.13(b): Information Security Standards

State of Texas law that sets forth the requirements state entities must follow regarding computer security.

Texas Penal Code, Chapter 33: Computer Crimes

State of Texas law specifically pertaining to computer crimes. Among other requirements, unauthorized use of University computers or unauthorized access to stored data, or dissemination of passwords or other confidential information to gain access to the University's computer system or data is in violation of criminal law.

Texas Penal Code, Chapter 37: Tampering with Governmental Record

Any alteration, destruction, or false entry of data that impairs the validity, legibility or availability of any record maintained by the University is a violation of criminal law.

United States Penal Code, Title 18, Section 1030: Fraud and related activity in connection with computers

Federal law specifically pertaining to computer crimes. Among other requirements, prohibits unauthorized and fraudulent access.

Federal Copyright Law

Recognizes that all intellectual works are automatically covered by copyright. The owner of a copyright holds the exclusive right to reproduce and distribute the work.

Links that may be useful:
http://library.tamu.edu/direct/reserve/Copyrightpolicy.html
http://www.utsystem.edu/ogc/intellectualproperty/cprtindx.htm

Computer Fraud and Abuse Act of 1986

Makes it a crime to access a computer to obtain restricted information without authorization; to alter, damage, or destroy information on a government computer; and to traffic in passwords or similar information used to gain unauthorized access to a government computer.

Electronic Communications Privacy Act of 1986

Prohibits the interception or disclosure of electronic communication and defines those situations in which disclosure is legal.

Computer Software Rental Amendments Act of 1990

Deals with the unauthorized rental, lease, or lending of copyrighted software.

Examples of Common Computing Violations

We hope that the table below will provide you with specific information you need to use the Tarleton computing resources responsibly.

Types of Violations
Abuse of Technology Resources:
Disruptive or mass mailings (mail bombing).
Disruptive print jobs.
Tying up workstations.

Adding a hub to the existing network.
Installing a web server or other server to provide applications, software, or files (e.g., BBS, Chat, DHCP, DNS, FTP, IRC, NTP, NNTP, POP2/3, SMTP, or WINS) on your microcomputer
Destroying or altering data or programs belonging to others (virus planting).
Improper Use of Accounts:
Chain letters and "Make Money Fast" schemes.
Message to all faculty and staff for non-business use; i.e., giving away free kittens or selling a sofa.
Commercial use of resources for personal gain.
Permitting another individual to use your account.
Using someone else's account.
Misappropriation of Intellectual Property:
Owning unlicensed copies of copyrighted materials (software & MP3 piracy).
Distribution of unlicensed copies of copyrighted material (software, MP3, etc.).
Invasion of Privacy:
Password cracking.
Network sniffing.
Unauthorized access to files and programs.
Harassment:
Using electronic communications to create a hostile work or learning environment.
Impersonating other individuals electronically.
Restricting access/denial of service.

Disclaimer: Other policies, laws, procedures, etc. may exist which cover these and other areas of technology use. It is not the intention of this list to be the only source of such information. Current TAMUS and Tarleton rules, regulations, and policies will control any infraction regardless of what may appear on these pages.

University Maintained Distribution Lists

The University provides and maintains these distribution lists:

Students	all students
Faculty	all faculty

Staff	all staff
k_students	Killeen students
k_faculty	Killeen faculty
k_staff	Killeen staff
s_students	Stephenville students
s_faculty	Stephenville faculty
s_staff	Stephenville staff

These lists allow the University to distribute information quickly but consume university resources and time. It is important to use these lists prudently and for university-related information only.

Please do not use the faculty, staff and students lists for:

Personal messages
Chain or mass-forwarded messages
Commercial messages, particularly item for sale or give-away
Large graphic files
Anything unrelated to the business of the university

University Approved Channels for Personal Communication

A bulletin board is available at http://www.tarleton.edu/main/bb/ for personal communication and non-business related messages.

There is a list serve, l_students, for open communication among students. Students may subscribe and unsubscribe to this list as desired.

To subscribe, send a mail message to mailserv@tarleton.edu:
Subject can be anything.
Text of the message: subscribe l_students username@tarleton.edu

To unsubscribe, send a mail message to mailserv@tarleton.edu:
Subject can be anything.
Text of the message: unsubscribe l_students username@tarleton.edu

You should receive confirmation of your request. Please contact the Help Desk at 968-9885 if you need further assistance.

Please remember that any commercial use of state resources is against both the Tarleton and The Texas A & M University System policies.

COMPUTER AND NETWORK ACCEPTABLE USE POLICY
UNIVERSITY OF PUGET SOUND

This Computer and Network Acceptable Use Policy outlines the responsibilities of student, faculty, and staff users of University-owned computing and network services and facilities. The University has an interest in providing Internet access and network accounts primarily to support its academic programs and administration of the University. This interest implies some constraints for members of the University community.

The Office of Information Systems (OIS) is responsible for operating the University's computing and network services. The goal of the OIS staff is to provide a high level of service to the campus community by maintaining access to a reliable and secure working environment in which files and messages on network servers are protected and regularly backed up by computing staff. In the normal course of system administration, the staff may need to access files, mail, and printed documents to diagnose and correct technical problems.

Students, faculty, and staff have a general responsibility to use campus computing and network services and facilities lawfully and in accordance with University standards of conduct as described in the University Integrity Code, Academic Honesty Policy, Sexual Harassment Policy, and other policies applicable to students, faculty, or staff. The following guidelines further pertain to the appropriate use of campus computing and network services.

1. **Threats, Harassment.** Users may not use campus computing or network services to threaten, harass, defame, or otherwise interfere with the legal rights of others.

2. **Respect for Privacy.** Users must respect the privacy of other users. Examples of lack of respect for the privacy of others include reading their mail, accessing their files, or using their computer account or electronic mail address (except as may be required in the case of University employees for the purpose of facilitating official University business).

3. **Sharing of Access.** Users may not share their password with others or let others use their account(s). Under no circumstances may users give others access to University systems.

4. **Academic Honesty.** Users must respect the intellectual property of others and adhere to University standards of academic honesty. Examples of academic dishonesty include accessing or using the files of others without their permission, altering or destroying their files or messages, violating standard citation requirements for information accessible electronically, or using copyrighted software or other copyrighted material in violation of the copyright agreement.

5. **Illegal Uses.** Users may not use computing or network services for illegal or other inappropriate purposes. Examples of illegal use include using University computers or the network to gain unauthorized access to other systems or to copy software or other materials protected by copyright law. Examples of other inappropriate uses include using campus computers or the network for commercial purposes, such as using the network to advertise a product or charging someone to use your account for network access.

6. **System Disruption.** Users must not intentionally disrupt the campus computing system or obstruct the work of other users, such as by interfering with the accounts of others, introducing or spreading viruses or other destructive programs on computers or the network, sending chain letters or blanket e-mail messages, or knowingly consuming inordinately large amounts of system resources.

7. **Operational Procedures.** Users must respect the University's operational procedures for computing and network services and facilities. Users are responsible for knowing and abiding by posted computer lab and network procedures. Generally, operational procedures prohibit printing multiple copies of documents on networked printers, playing games in labs when others are waiting for systems, or using interactive utilities such as ICQ on dial-in lines. Finally, as instructional use is paramount, users must leave a lab when it is needed by a class that has reserved the room in advance.

Failure to comply with these guidelines may result in the denial of access to campus computing or network services, and may further subject the user to disciplinary action. Computing staff may directly address violations of this policy or refer them to the Associate Dean for Student Development, Academic Vice President, or Director of Human Resources, as appropriate.

The staff of the Office of Information Systems will respond as appropriate to complaints of harassment or other misuse of computing and network services. To register a complaint or raise a concern, contact the Manager of Network Services, or the Director of Instructional Technology and Training.

June 1996; rev. August 1997; rev. April 2000

University of Richmond| Information Services

Policies for Responsible Computing

The following University of Richmond policies apply to the entire university community. The policies address the responsible use of information and technology resources, violations of policy and guidelines for effective use of technology resources. Individuals are also subject to federal, state and local laws governing many interactions that occur on the Internet. These policies and guidelines are subject to change as state and federal laws develop and change. Suggestions on these policies are welcomed and should be sent to the Vice President for Information Services at epolicy@richmond.edu.

Contents:

I. The University of Richmond's Policy on Responsible Computing

Everyone within the University of Richmond community who uses University computing and network facilities has the responsibility to use them in an ethical, professional, and legal manner.

This means that users agree to abide by the following

conditions:

- Use the University 's computing facilities and information resources, including hardware, software, networks, and computer accounts, responsibly and appropriately. Respect the rights of other computing users, and respect all contractual and license agreements.
- Use only those computers and computer accounts for which you have authorization.
- The University's network and computer infrastructure is a finite resource. Use computer accounts for the purpose(s) for which they have been issued. Use University-owned microcomputers and advanced workstations for University-related projects only. Commercial use of the University's computing resources, not related to the academic, research, and scholarly pursuits is prohibited.
- Be responsible for all computer accounts and for protecting each account's password. In other words, do not share computer accounts. If someone else learns your password, you must change it.
- Report unauthorized use of your accounts to your project director, instructor, supervisor, system administrator, or other appropriate University authority.
- During an investigation of a problem, cooperate with Information Services' requests for information about computing activities.
- Do not participate in the malicious use of computing resources.
- Report any abuse of computing resources to epolicy@richmond.edu.

II. Computing Violations

Examples of prohibited actions (not a comprehensive list) that are subject to disciplinary review are:

- Attacking the security of the system or failing to maintain the security of the system;
- Using obscene or abusive language in electronic communications;
- Harassing, threatening or otherwise causing harm to specific individuals, e.g. sending an individual repeated and unwanted (harassing) email or using email to threaten or stalk someone
- Accessing or attempting to access another individual's

data or information without proper authorization, e.g. running an unauthorized remote control of another's computer;

- Tapping phone or network lines, e.g. running network sniffers without authorization;
- Releasing a virus, worm or other program that damages or harms a system or network;
- Preventing others from accessing services;
- Sending pyramid or chain letters over the network;
- Accessing data or files without authorization, even if they are not securely protected, e.g. taking advantage of security holes;
- Modifying or divulging private information such as electronic files or the contents of mail without the consent of the owner of the files;
- Using or misusing of University electronic data without authorization;
- Modifying, damaging, defacing, moving or destroying data which does not belong to you;
- Using the national network, the internet, in a manner contrary to established guidelines and laws;
- Downloading or posting to university computers, or transporting across the university networks, material that is illegal, proprietary, in violation of university contracts, or otherwise damaging to the institution, e.g. launching a computer virus, distributing child pornography via the web, posting copyright or contract protected information.
- Violations of federal, state, or local laws.

The underlying premise of the above policy is:

The legitimate use of a computer or a network does not extend to whatever an individual is capable of doing with it. Just because a person is able to circumvent restrictions and security, this does not mean that the person is allowed to do so.

III. The University of Richmond Policy and Procedures on Handling Violations

The primary responsibilities of Information Services are neither investigative nor disciplinary; however, in cases where University resources and privileges are abused or otherwise threatened, the staff in the offices will take appropriate steps.

- In all cases where a member of the University community allegedly has committed one of the above violations, Information Services will immediately revoke access privileges pending the outcome of a full review of the problem.
- The person will be notified as quickly as possible, by phone, electronic, campus or U.S. mail of the alleged violation. A representative of the Information Services Security Team will contact the person to propose a meeting to discuss the alleged violation.
- If the issue cannot be resolved, and depending on the nature of the alleged offense, Information Services will contact the appropriate senior university administrator (Director of Human Resources, Dean, Vice President, Campus Police) or law enforcement agencies alerting them of the alleged violation and conferring on the proper next steps.
- *In all cases, if the problem in question overlaps with another disciplinary or law enforcement process, this process will defer to the other. In such cases, interim revocations by system administrators may remain in effect until the other process has been completed.*
- Once a formal complaint is made, the University shall protect the confidentiality of those involved to the extent permitted by law and to the extent that continued protection does not interfere with the University's ability to investigate allegations and to take corrective action.
- Because Information Services staff have access to systems and information that extends into many areas of the university, and because the university community must trust Information Services staff to treat its systems and information with the utmost integrity and confidentiality, if an Information Services staff member allegedly commits one of the above violations, the following process will be followed:
  - o Pending the outcome of the discovery, the staff member will be immediately suspended with pay and all computer and network access will be revoked. The only employees who will have knowledge of the discovery and suspension will be those who need to assist in the discovery process and in the network and systems security procedures.
  - o If the investigation determines that the staff member committed the violation, the staff member will be terminated immediately. The University's progressive disciplinary process does not apply to

    these types of violations.
- o If the investigation determines that no offense was committed, the staff member will be immediately removed from suspension and will return to their job with no record of a personnel action in their file.

IV. The University of Richmond's Software and Intellectual Property Copyright Policy

- **Federal copyright laws** protect the software available for use on computers at the University of Richmond. Educational institutions are not exempt from the laws covering copyright. In addition, software is normally protected by a license agreement between the purchaser and the software seller. The software provided through the University for use by faculty, staff, and students may be used only on computing equipment as specified in the various software licenses.
- **It is University policy** to respect the copyright protections given to software and intellectual property owners by federal law. It is against University policy for faculty, staff, or students to copy or reproduce any licensed software or intellectual property on University computing equipment, except as expressly permitted by the software license or granting authority. Faculty, staff, and students may not use copies of software that have been obtained illegally on University-owned computers or on personal computers housed in University facilities.
- **Unauthorized use of software** is illegal and is regarded as a serious matter and any such use is without the consent of the University of Richmond and is subject to disciplinary action by the appropriate division in the university.

V. E-mail Guidelines: Privacy and Etiquette

Faculty, staff, and students can expect that the e-mail messages are treated confidentially because the University does not monitor employees' or students' e-mail transactions. However, e-mail messages are written records that could be subject to review with just cause. Courts have also ruled that e-mail records and information in electronic form on central computers can be subpoenaed in some cases. Under present circumstances, the privacy of e-mail cannot be guaranteed.

University policy establishes the privacy of the messages and the files on the central computers. Be aware, however, when we experience system problems, such as hardware or software failure or attacks by malicious users, the staff who maintain the mail servers are authorized to look at any information and any files on university computers that are necessary to solve the problems and to protect the systems and the information they contain. It is part of the system administrator's job to do this and to treat any information on the systems as confidential.

While the University respects faculty, staff and students privacy to all reasonable limits, the University and/or Information Services cannot guarantee that all email will remain private. In addition to the authorized actions of system administrators, e-mail can end up in the hands of computing staff if it was inaccurately addressed and if it could not be delivered. People also make small mistakes in addressing their mail so that private messages appear in the mailbox of someone other than the intended recipient.

University policies prohibit certain kinds of e-mail messages. Policies prohibit using email for harassment, political campaigning, and solicitation. Chain mail is an irresponsible use of resources, and it taxes the network; therefore, sending chain mail is a violation of policy.

Some hints and guidelines on email:

- Just like written letters, the e-mail messages are owned by the receiver. They can easily be redistributed or copied by the recipients.
- Realize that University policy and secure passwords provide good but not complete assurance of the privacy of e-mail messages. When the confidentiality of a message is of the utmost importance, only a person-to-person conversation may be sufficiently secure.
- Delete messages that should not be preserved.
- Resist the temptation to send chain mail, even when it promises you fame and fortune. A message that has been forwarded ten or more times is a chain letter. This is a waste of computing resources, it's a nuisance, and it often offends recipients.
- Don't use University resources, computing or otherwise, for political campaigning or soliciting.

VI. Securing Passwords; Protecting Files; Protecting University Information

Many systems at the University require the use of passwords. These include email, the Web, labs in Jepson, the modem pool (when dialing in from off campus), and others. Although each of these systems has its own requirements, they all share the requirement that passwords be kept protected to prevent any unauthorized use.

The Importance of Password Protection

Your login ID and password authenticate you as an authorized user of the University of Richmond's computing environment. A good password policy is key to the University's overall systems security. You need to protect your own files and University resources by choosing a good password and protecting it.

If another person discovers your password, that individual potentially has access to your email, your personal files, and your online network identity and accounts. A knowledgeable person could use your account to illegally gain access to other network resources putting them at risk. Part of a strong defense against intruders is a good secure password.

Hackers often gain access to a system by "cracking" accounts. They use automated processes to guess passwords. This process is quick and easy for them if you use a dictionary word or your login ID for a password. You should change your password regularly, at least once a semester. You should change your password immediately if you notice unusual activity on your system or account. If you suspect that someone is illegally accessing computing resources using your identity please contact the IS Help Desk at extension 6400 or report it to abuse@richmond.edu.

It is important that you choose a good password and keep is secret from everyone. No one should be given your password -- not even someone from Information Services.

Information Services may run a program from time to time that looks across our systems for crackable passwords. If we find one on your account we will ask you to change it immediately. We will also put procedures in place that will prevent users from selecting insecure passwords where possible.

If passwords are created intelligently and kept protected, the danger is minimized; but if an employee is not careful to protect his or her password, that employee can permit an unscrupulous person access to a valuable University asset: its information.

How to Choose a Good Password

The University's policy for choosing a good (that is, less hackable) password requires the following for all systems:

- Do not use "dictionary words" (even if they are "disguised" by capital letters or numbers, like 'RiCHmonD' or 'birthday98'), foreign words, names, dates, phone numbers or anything else someone might be able to simply guess or determine using a hacking tool.
- Use six to eight characters. Using more may not work with the system you are using, and using less makes the password too easy to hack or guess. Use at least two letters and at least one non-letter (number or special character), but the first character in the password must be a letter.
- Make your password easy for you to remember, but hard for someone else to guess. Picking letters from a phrase that's meaningful to you may make a good password. An example could be "Fall 98 classes begin on August 25" becomes f9cboA2.
- Intersperse numbers, punctuation marks and special characters. Allowable special characters are: @ # $ % ^ & * ( ) _ - + = { } [ ] \ : ; " ? ' / > . < and ,
- Use a unique password. Do not use one that you are using for some other purpose, such as your PIN at your bank or your password to another University system.

How to Protect Your Password

- You should never write your password down! However, if you must write it down be sure to store it where no one else will see it.
- Do not put it on or near your computer, in the front of your Rolodex (or filed under "P"), or in your desk drawer. Put it somewhere where no one but you will have access to it, such as in your wallet. There is no reason for anyone but you to ever have access to your passwords, so there is no reason to share them with

anyone in your office.
- Change your password occasionally. Change it when:
  - You have never changed it from the default password used initially;
  - You have told it to anyone, or have written it down and think it may have been observed;
  - You have used the same password for more than six months;
  - Your password does not meet the criteria for a good password in this policy;
  - You are advised by IS or your system administrator to change it;
  - You have reason to suspect the password has been compromised.

Special Rules for the Modem Pool

If you log on through the University's Modem Pool from home, you must keep your password secure, just as you do at work. Any inappropriate use of University resources (for example keeping the modem connection open for long periods of time, or using the login to attempt to "hack" University or other systems) using your login will be considered your responsibility. For this reason it is imperative that the password be kept secret and secure.

If You Forget your Password

Contact the Help Desk at extension 6400; new procedures are coming to make this easier and more secure.

VII. The University of Richmond Statement on Obscene Material

While the University of Richmond is a private university, all members of the community still must observe state and federal laws. Although it may be difficult to draw the line in determining what is or is not obscene, students, faculty and staff should know that Virginia Code Section 18.2-372 defines "obscene" as that which:

> *"Considered as a whole, has as its dominant theme or purpose . . . a shameful or morbid interest in nudity, sexual conduct, sexual excitement, excretory functions or products*

*thereof or sadomasochistic abuse, and which goes
substantially beyond customary limits of candor in
description or representation of such matters and
which, taken as a whole, does not have serious
literary, artistic, political, or scientific value."*

The distribution, production, publication or sale of obscene
items is illegal in Virginia (Va. Code Section 18.2-374). A first
offense is punishable as a Class 1 misdemeanor that carries a
sentence of up to twelve months in jail and/or a fine of not
more than $2,500. Any subsequent obscenity conviction is a
Class 6 felony that carries a sentence of between one and five
years in prison, or up to twelve months in jail and/or a fine of
$2,500.

Further, a student, faculty or staff member distributing obscene
material through a web page or other means could be subject to
criminal prosecution in other states to the extent that any
individual in those states accesses the web page or other
delivery mechanism. Such action may violate federal law as
well (18 U.S.C. Section 1465) which makes the transportation
of obscene materials in interstate commerce a criminal act.
Conviction under federal law can result in a prison sentence of
up to five years, a fine of not more than $5,000, or both.

In addition, placing obscene material on a University of
Richmond server violates University policies, including but not
limited to the computer usage policy as well as employee and
student standards of conduct. Such violations will result in
disciplinary actions.

VIII. University Technology Resources: Ownership

The University owns the central computers, computer labs, the
micro-computing sites, and the computers it places on its staff
and faculty desks and all the software it has installed on them.
The University owns the campus network - all wires, cables,
and routers that connect the personal computers, central
computers, computer labs, microcomputer sites, and servers to
each other and to the Internet. The University 's division of
Information Services determines who is authorized to use its
network.

While the University of Richmond owns the computers in all
the offices and departments, each individual staff member

makes the decision about how that equipment will be used. The University also owns the software licenses (word processing, spreadsheet software, email, etc.) that were purchased from a software vendor using university funds. The licenses usually allow ONE copy of this software per workstation..

Also, although the University considers your mail and files private, it can't give unlimited space to store them. Cleaning out mailboxes is a task that should be practiced regularly.

IX. Foreign Invaders: Viruses

Computer viruses are segments of program code that interfere with the running of the programs and with access to data on a computer. The virus code resides on a diskette or on another computer system on a network. When the virus code is copied from the diskette or from another computer system over the network, it infects the system it is copied onto.

In 1988, there were less than a dozen computer viruses in existence. There are now over 21,000 known viruses attacking personal computers.

Many viruses are more of a nuisance than an actual cause of damage to the computer system or data. One virus simply prints "Don't panic" on the screen. Many other viruses, however, destroy data and render computer systems inoperable. The Michelangelo virus overwrites the hard disk. The Jerusalem virus deletes executable files. Some viruses called "rabbits" just reproduce, eventually taking up all processor capacity, memory, and disk, denying the user access to system resources. Word processor and spreadsheet macro viruses are another threat. Some viruses serve as Trojan Horses and open your computer up to external and illegal users.

Installing or knowingly proliferating viruses in any format is a serious violation of university policy and is subject to disciplinary action by the appropriate authorities in the university.

Hints and guidelines on computer viruses:

- Be suspicious of freeware and shareware. Be wary of downloading files from electronic bulletin boards.
- Back up, store, and routinely check backup copies of all

files and programs. Keep the backups for as long as six months to a year.

- **Use anti-virus software. For Windows computers, anti-virus software is available at no cost to University of Richmond faculty, staff, and students from the Help Desk.**

X. What to do if You are a Victim of Computer Abuse, Harassment or Irresponsible Behavior

Unfortunately computer abuse, harassment, malicious behavior, and unauthorized account access do happen. If you are a victim of computer abuse, report the violations to, the Dean of your college, your supervisor, the Campus Police or Information Services at epolicy@richmond.edu. Sending a message to epolicy will alert the Vice President or a senior member of the Information Services staff to your situation. Please keep copies of the harassing e-mail messages, dates, and times of unauthorized access, etc., for investigative purposes. Cases are handled individually and in the utmost confidentiality.

The University shall protect the confidentiality of those involved to the extent permitted by law and to the extent that continued protection does not interfere with the University's ability to investigate allegations and to take corrective action.

UNIVERSITY OF
SOUTHERN COLORADO

University of Southern Colorado
Electronic Communication Policy

I. Purpose

II. Definition

III. Electronic Communication Policy
   A. Ownership of Electronic Communication and Permissible Uses
   B. Prohibited Uses
   C. University Access and Disclosure
   D. Disciplinary Action
   E. Electronic Communication Privacy
   F. System Conservation

I. Purpose

To guide usage of all forms of electronic communication.

Back to the Top

II. Definition

For purposes of this policy statement, electronic communications includes but is not limited to electronic mail, Internet services, voice mail, audio and video conferencing, and facsimile messages that are sent or received by faculty, staff, students, and other authorized users of university resources.

Back to the Top

III. Policy

    A. Ownership of Electronic Communication and Permissible Uses

The University provides various forms of electronic communications for the purposes of conducting academic pursuits and other university business. The records created are the property of the University, not of the individuals sending or receiving such messages. Authorization to utilize electronic and voice mail is established by the Computer Center with right of appeal to the Office of the Provost. Individuals who are authorized to use electronic and voice mail may make incidental and occasional personal use of these facilities when such use does not generate a direct cost to the University. In doing so, users acknowledge the organization's ownership of the systems and its rights with regard to use.

Back to the Top

    B. Prohibited Uses

Prohibited uses include but are not limited to:
1. Commercial purposes or other personal gain.
2. Use of electronic communications to send copies of documents in violation of copyright laws.
3. The transmission of information, access to which is restricted by laws or regulations.
4. Use of electronic communications to intimidate, threaten, or harass other individuals, or to interfere with the ability of others to conduct university business.
5. The forging of communication so it appears to be from someone else.
6. Obtaining or attempting to obtain access to data, files, other electronic communication, etc. other than that for which one has proper authorization. Any attempt to breach security measures to access or acquire any electronically stored information one is not authorized to obtain is prohibited. These acts are prohibited regardless of methods

utilized.

The term "access" includes reading, deleting, moving, changing access privileges, or affecting files, data, etc. in any unauthorized manner.

7. Use of chain letters.
8. Electronic communications conduct is expected to meet the standards of conduct, laws, regulations, etc. published in official University, State or Federal documents including but not limited to the USC catalog, the Faculty Handbook, Colorado State Employees Handbook, etc.

Back to the Top

C. University Access and Disclosure

The contents of e-mail messages, backups, and archives may be required to be disclosed as a result of legal discovery, writ, warrant or subpoena, or as a result of a request under the Colorado Open Records Law. E-mail is not backed up by the Computer Center. The University will not monitor electronic communication as a routine matter. Message contents will be inspected as needed to protect health and safety or security.

Back to the Top

D. Disciplinary Action

If a violation of policy is suspected, the Computer Center staff will refer the matter to appropriate authorities such as the University Police, the Provost's Office, the Personnel Office, and the Dean of Student Services. If a condition exists where Computer Center personnel feel there is a need for immediate action, that action (account deactivation, etc.) will be taken, then the matter referred to the authorities listed above. These cases will be limited to instances involving safety, security, or another matter of an emergency nature.

Back to the Top

E. Electronic Communication Privacy

E-mail is not like a phone call. More information, including copies of the content of your messages, is routinely recorded about the use of e-mail than about your use of the telephone. A broader, less controlled set of people have access to that information.

E-mail is not like a letter in an envelope, and there's no easy way to mark a message "confidential." E-mail is most like a postcard. The contents of your message may be viewed during the mailing process. If there is a problem with routing, a "postmaster" may read your message to try to redirect it correctly. Your message can be forwarded or printed.

Don't put anything in an e-mail message that is not for public inspection. Do use professional, courteous language. It's much easier to edit a message before you send it, than to send an apology. If you receive mail that was not intended for you, send an appropriate reply to the sender.

Back to the Top

F. System Conservation

Help conserve e-mail resources. If the system is used for trivia, it won't be available for other, more worthwhile uses. Never send junk mail or "Who are you?" messages.

Limit your use of lists as much as possible. Many of the global e-mail lists are available in other forms such as the World Wide Web. If you subscribe to a list, always make sure that you know how to unsubscribe from that list, and do so when you no longer have a use for the information from the list, or when you are going away from the University for an extended time.

Be careful when sending e-mail lists. Sending large messages to lists that may have hundreds of users can dramatically impact both the e-mail system you are using to send the message and the e-mail systems receiving the message.

Before sending to any list or replying to any message from a list, make sure that you know the guidelines and policies of that list and that you are aware of where your message is going (to the whole list, or just the person that sent the original message).

To conserve disk space, the Computer Center will purge e-mail messages over one year old. Users wishing to retain messages past that time frame should save messages to the network, their hard drive, or to floppies.

Back to the Top

Effective: July 1, 1996

Resources - Computer Services

Resources

Back to
Computer Services

Computer Usage Policy

**Upper Iowa University
Computer Use Policy**

Computer use among faculty, staff and students at Upper Iowa University is restricted to purposes consistent with the stated mission of the University. The University's computing resources are to be used in an ethical, courteous, and fair manner for the following purposes:

- Class assignments
- Academic research and investigation
- Computing for personal and professional advancement
- Administrative and instructional support
- Staff and faculty consulting (subject to provisions contained in relevant personnel policy).

Use of Upper Iowa University computing facilities is restricted to current employees and students, to ensure compliance with acceptable use policies of the Internet and to maintain the security of administrative computing systems. On a case-by-case basis, the Director of Computer Services may grant access to individuals employed by non-profit agencies or to family members of Upper Iowa employees. **System resources such as network servers, processor performance, and disk space are routinely monitored by Computer Services personnel to ensure system security and integrity. Anyone using shared computing facilities at Upper Iowa University implicitly consents to such monitoring by authorized personnel.**

The Upper Iowa University campus network includes campus-based computer systems, wide-area networks (WANs), local-area networks (LANs), telecommunications equipment, and the high-speed network linking the campus to the Iowa Communications Network and the worldwide Internet. Upper Iowa University computer users must not engage in unauthorized or inappropriate conduct on the Internet or Upper Iowa University WAN/LAN networks or facilities. Examples of such activities include:

- Using or sharing another person's log-in ID to access computing facilities at Upper Iowa University or another Internet facility. This includes permitting others to use your own log-in ID.
- Using Upper Iowa University facilities to crack or access systems, whether

on campus or off, in an unauthorized or inappropriate manner.

- Using Upper Iowa University networking facilities to engage in illegal or criminal activities.
- Using Upper Iowa University networking facilities to threaten or harass another person.
- Attempting to read or access another person's electronic mail or other protected files.
- Copying or distributing software that violates copyright laws, license agreements, and intellectual property, as outlined in the Copyright Law of the United States of America, revised March 1, 1989, in Title 17 of the United States Code, Section 117.
- Establishing personal World Wide Web pages for off-campus access without authorization.
- Knowingly distributing or actively developing a computer virus, worm, or Trojan Horse.
- Repeated use of Upper Iowa University networked facilities in a discourteous manner, including: using excessive amounts of system resources (e.g., CPU time ban width or disk space), thereby preventing access by other users; consuming excessive volumes of printing resources; sending unwelcome electronic mail messages and posting information to public folders that is inappropriate or irrelevant to the intended subject area; disturbing others while using public-access computing laboratories; refusing to yield workstations in public labs to users for activities of higher priority; and engagement in activities such as forwarding chain mail.

Computer resources have been allocated for World Wide Web activities that support research, education, administrative processes, and other legitimate pursuits. All activities must be consistent with this purpose. Violations include, but are not limited to:

- Commercial activities
- Creating, displaying, or transmitting threatening, racist, sexist, obscene, or harassing language and/or materials
- Games not related to Upper Iowa University programs and/or mission
- Copyright and licensing violations
- Violation of personal privacy
- Vandalism and mischief that incapacitates, compromises, or destroys University resources and/or violates federal and/or state laws.

Examples of such violations include commercial advertising; displaying pornography or racist jokes; providing copies of software that is not in the public domain; posting private personal information without permission such as grades, medical records, or any other information that is protected by the Public Records Law; and providing information or instructions to compromise University security measures.

Electronic Mail

System administrators are expected to treat the contents of electronic files as private and confidential. Inspection of electronic files and electronic mail, and any action based upon such inspection, will be governed by all applicable federal and Iowa laws. The Upper Iowa University community is advised that all files stored on main systems, including electronic mail, are backed up regularly and may be subject to subpoena.

Enforcement of policies

Upper Iowa University supports activities that adhere to high academic standards and respect for personal and public resources. You are the first line of enforcement. Think before you act and understand the consequences of your actions. If you have any questions, please contact the Computer Services Office at 563-425-5308.

Violators of these rules are subject to disciplinary action in accordance with relevant University policies and procedures.

University responsibilities

The Director of Computer Services has a responsibility to enforce, within reasonable limits, University policies regulating computer use. In order to determine whether violations of regulations are occurring, the computer services team may monitor user activity on the Upper Iowa University network, either randomly or systematically. An account may be systematically monitored only when there is documented reason (such as the results of random monitoring or the written complaint of a user) to believe activity in the account is in violation o University policy. The content of files stored on networked devices may be inspected only with the express consent of the Director of Computer Services and only for the purpose of determining whether violations of policy have occurred.

Sanctions for violation of regulations

Decisions to temporarily or permanently limit, suspend, or revoke computer privileges of users found to be in violation of Upper Iowa University computer policies will be made only with the concurrence of the Senior Vice President for Residential University, Senior Vice President for Extended University, or Senior Vice President for Business Services (as appropriate to the status of the person whose account is being restricted). Additionally, these administrators will be notified of violations of computer policy that may also constitute violations o other University policies, such as harassment.

UPPER IOWA UNIVERSITY

Residential Campus | Regional Learning Centers | Online Program | External Degree

Wartburg College Computing Policies

Effective July 1, 1996

Computer use is encouraged among faculty, staff, and students at Wartburg College for purposes consistent with the stated mission of the college. Wartburg College is dedicated to challenging and nurturing students for lives of leadership and service as a spirited expression of their faith and learning. As a consequence, Wartburg Computing resources are to be used in an ethical, courteous, and fair manner for the following purposes:

- class assignments
- academic research and investigation
- computing for personal and professional advancement
- administrative and instructional support
- staff and faculty consulting subject to provisions contained in relevant personnel policy

Use of Wartburg College computing facilities is restricted to current employees and students to ensure compliance with acceptable use policies of the Internet and maintain the security of administrative computing systems. On a case by case basis the Director of Computing Services may grant access to individuals employed by non-profit agencies or family members of Wartburg employees. System resources such as processor performance and disk space are routinely monitored by Computer Services personnel to ensure system security and integrity. Anyone using shared computing facilities at Wartburg College implicitly consents to such monitoring by authorized personnel.

The Wartburg Information Network (WINnet) includes campus-based computer systems, local-area networks, telecommunications equipment and the high-speed network linking the campus to the Iowa Communications Network and the world-wide Internet. Wartburg computer users must not engage in unauthorized or inappropriate conduct on the Internet or WINnet facilities. Examples of such activities include:

- Using or sharing another person's login id to access computing facilities at Wartburg or another Internet facility. This includes permitting others to use your own login id.
- Using WINnet facilities to crack or access systems, whether on campus or off, in an unauthorized or inappropriate manner.
- Using WINnet facilities to engage in illegal or criminal activities.
- Using WINnet facilities to threaten or harass another person.
- Attempting to read or access another person's electronic mail or other protected files.
- Copying or distributing software which violates copyright laws, license agreements, and intellectual property as outlined in the *Copyright Law of the United States of America*, revised March 1, 1989 in Title 17 of the United States Code, Section 117.
- Establishing personal world-wide web pages for off campus access without authorization.
- Knowingly distributing or actively developing a computer virus, worm, or Trojan Horse.

Repeated use of WINnet facilities in a discourteous manner including:

- using excessive amounts of system resources (e.g. CPU time or disk space) thereby preventing access by other users;

- consuming excessive volumes of printing resources;
- sending unwelcome electronic mail messages and posting information to USENET news groups which are inappropriate or irrelevant to the intended subject area;
- disturbing others while using public access computing laboratories;
- refusing to yield workstations in public labs to users for activities of higher priority.

Violation of these policies constitutes computer abuse and disciplinary actions will be governed by the Wartburg Student Conduct System. Computer abuse by employees of Wartburg College will be handled by appropriate administrative channels. Computer Services' role in the process will be to call attention to the situation, gather and validate pertinent information and forward the information to the appropriate Dean or Vice President. If abusive or discourteous use is traced to an off campus Internet host, remote system administrators shall be contacted immediately. Violations of courtesy are to be referred to the Director of Computing Services or designee.

Electronic Mail

System administrators are expected to treat the contents of electronic files as private and confidential. Inspection of electronic files and electronic mail, and any action based upon such inspection, will be governed by all applicable U. S. and Iowa laws. The Wartburg community is advised that all files stored on main systems, including electronic mail, are backed-up regularly and may be subject to subpoena.

USENET News

USENET News is a strategic resource and an integral component of the teaching and learning environment of Wartburg college. Wartburg College Computer Services actively maintains a news server for the Wartburg community and does not restrict access to news groups based on content or subject matter. However, some news groups requiring resources that adversely affect general news access may be regulated by the Director of Computing Services or designee. Any news group may contain ideas or language considered objectionable by members of the Wartburg community. As such, it is understood that having such articles on the Wartburg College news server does not constitute an endorsement of the ideas presented nor acceptance of the language or material in the articles. Members of the Wartburg community who actively participate in USENET news discussions are requested to include disclaimers confirming their postings do not represent official statements of Wartburg College.

World-Wide Web

Computer Services actively maintains a World-Wide Web (WWW) server for the Wartburg Community with College Relations holding primary responsibility and authority over web pages containing official campus information. Wartburg College recognizes the value and potential of publishing on the Internet, and so allows and encourages students, staff, and faculty to publish electronic information via the world-wide web within the guidelines posted on the Wartburg WWW Server. Academic and Administrative units may create web pages to carry out the college's stated mission. Content of these WWW pages must be consistent with college policy including policies and standards for print publications.

Wartburg College

Individual faculty, staff, and students may create personal web pages hosted on the campus WWW server only after affirming their acceptance of college computing policies and guidelines by signing forms at Computer Services. A personal page may be in violation if it contains links to pages that violate college policy. Each personal, departmental, and student organization WWW page must include appropriate disclaimers as specified in guidelines on file in Computer Services.

Effective July 1, 1996

[Resources] [Labs] [Support Documents][Workshops][Personnel][Wartburg][Search]

Maintained By: Thomas L. Hausmann, Director of Academic Computing, hausmann@wartburg.edu

Last Modified Tuesday, September 8, 1998

Copyright by Wartburg College

Computer Use and Abuse Policy

West Virginia State College has established policies regarding the use or abuse of all hardware, data, software and communications networks associated with campus computer systems.

WVSC users are also subject to applicable network (BITNET, Internet, etc.) usage guidelines, as well as state and federal laws regarding computer abuse. The "West Virginia Computer Crime and Abuse Act," which defines computer abuse and prosecution possibilities, went into effect July, 1989. The Electronic Communications Privacy Act, passed by Congress in 1986, cites illegal electronic communications access and interception. Cases of computer abuse must be reported to the appropriate WVSC Computer Services personnel and/or to local, state and federal authorities.

Common Forms of Computer Abuse

West Virginia State College is responsible for informing users of the rules, regulations and procedures which apply when using network computing resources. Users are responsible for understanding these rules so that they can abide by them. These policies cover West Virginia State College as well as WVNET services.

Privacy

Investigating or reading another user's file is considered a violation of privacy. Reading unprotected files is intrusive; reading protected files, by whatever mechanism, is considered the same as "breaking and entering." Violations include:

- Attempting to access another user's files without permission.
- Furnishing false or misleading information or identification in order to access another user's account.
- Attempts to access WVSC's computers, computer facilities, networks, systems, programs or data without authorization.
- Unauthorized manipulation of WVSC's computer systems, programs or data.

Theft

Attempted or detected alteration of software, data or other files as well as disruption or destruction of equipment or resources is considered theft. Violations include:

- Using subterfuge to avoid being charged for computer resources.
- Deliberate, unauthorized use of another users' account to avoid being billed for computer use.

- Abusing specific resources such as BITNET or the Internet.
- Removing computer equipment (hardware, software, data, etc.) without authorization.
- Copying or attempting to copy data or software without authorization.

Vandalism

Violations include:

- Sending mail or a program which will replicate itself (such as a computer virus) or do damage to another user's account.
- Tampering with or obstructing the operation of WVSC's computer systems.
- Inspecting, modifying or distributing data or software (or attempting to do so) without authorization.
- Damaging computer hardware or software.

Harassment

Sending unwanted messages or files to other users may be considered harassment. Violations include:

- Interfering with legitimate work of another user.
- Sending abusive or obscene messages via computers.
- Using computer resources to engage in abuse of computer service personnel or other users.

Copyright Issues

West Virginia STate College prohibits the copying, transmitting, or disclosing of proprietary data, software or documentation (or attempting to commit these acts) without proper authorization.

Miscellaneous

Other acts considered unethical and abusive include:

- Unauthorized and time-consuming recreational game playing.
- Using computer accounts for work not authorized for that account.
- Sending chain letters or unauthorized mass mailings.
- Using the computer for personal profit or other illegal purposes.
- Personal advertisements.
- Display of offensive material and graphics in public areas.

Software and Intellectual Rights

Respect for intellectual labor and creativity is vital to academic discourse and enterprise. This principal applies to works of all authors and publishers in all media. It encompasses respect for the right to acknowledgement, right to privacy, and right to determine the form, manner, and terms of publications and distribution.

Because electronic information is volatile and easily reproduced, respect for the work and personal expression of others is especially critical in computer environments. Violations of authorial integrity, including plagiarism, invasion of privacy, unauthorized access, and trade secret or copyright violations may be grounds for sanctions against members of the academic community.

This Statement of Software and Intellectual Rights applies in full to the use of West Virginia State College Computer Services and its resources.

Computer Usage Guidelines

1. You must have a valid, authorized account and you may only use those computer resources for which you are specifically authorized. You are responsible for safeguarding your own account. You should not allow another user to use your account unless authorized by the system administrator for a specific purpose.
2. You may not change, copy, delete, read or otherwise access files or software without the permission of the owner or the system administrator. You may not bypass accounting or security mechanisms to circumvent data protection schemes. You may not attempt to modify software except when it is intended to be customized by users.
3. You may not prevent others from accessing the system, nor unreasonably slow down the system by deliberately running wasteful jobs, playing games, or engaging in non-productive or idle computer "chatting."
4. You should assume that any software you did not create is copyrighted. You may neither distribute copyrighted or proprietary material without the written consent of the copyright holder, nor violate copyright or patent laws concerning computer software, documentation or other tangible assets.
5. You must not use the West Virginia State College computer systems to violate any rules in the West Virginia State College Employee Handbook, or local, state or federal laws.
6. You should promptly report misuse of computing resources, or potential loopholes in computer systems security, to the appropriate authorities (WVSC Computer Services Director or Computer Services personnel), and cooperate with the systems administrators in their investigation of abuse.

In connection with inquiries into possible abuses, WVSC Computer Services reserves the right, with approval of the WVSC Computer

Services Director, to examine files, programs, passwords, accounting information, printouts, or other computing material without notice. Privacy of any electronic or printed material examined that is not relevant to the investigation is guaranteed. Disclosure of such material will be subject to penalty.

Penalties for Computer Abuse

Abuse or misuse of West Virginia State College computing facilities and services may not only be a violation of network policy and user responsibility, but it may also violate the criminal code. Therefore, West Virginia State College will take appropriate action in response to user abuse or misuse of computing facilities and services. Action may include, but is not necessarily limited to:

- Suspension or revocation of computing privileges. Access to all computing facilities and systems can, may or will be denied.
- Reimbursement to West Virginia State College or the appropriate institution for resources consumed.
- Other legal action including action to recover damages.
- Referral to law enforcement authorities.
- Referral of offending faculty, staff and/or students to institutional authorities for disciplinary action.

Information Technologies & Services

POLICIES : ACCEPTABLE USE POLICY

Acceptable Use
Policy (from Staff
Handbook)

Digital Millennium
Copyright Act

- - - - - - - - -

Quick Start Guides

**Support Center
x3900**

Education

ResNet

Banner x3410

**Network, Mail & File
Services**

Phones x4444

**Office Services &
Post Office**

**Computer Sales &
Repair**

Software Sources

- - - - - - - -

Department Directory

Policies

IT&S Home

ACCEPTABLE USE OF CAMPUS NETWORK AND COMPUTING SYSTEMS

This policy applies to students. The Staff Handbook contains the corresponding policy for faculty and staff.

In support of its educational mission Wheaton College provides a campus data network - including in-room connection services in all campus residence halls; computer systems - including electronic mail, file sharing, printing and world-wide web services; and other electronic services - including campus telephone services and cable television. It is the responsibility of each member of the community to use these services appropriately and in compliance with all College, City, County, State, and Federal laws and regulations. This policy covers all persons accessing a computer, telecommunications or network resource at Wheaton College.

The Honor Code and Wheaton Community Standards apply to use of the college's network and computing services. Actions that are unacceptable in other settings are also unacceptable on the network, computing systems and other electronic services, including:
· Harassment in any form.
· Failure to respect the property and rights of others.
· Forgery or other misrepresentation of one's identity.
· Distribution of copyrighted materials without the permission of the copyright owner.

In addition, these policies specific to Wheaton's network and electronic services apply:

· College systems and networks may only be used for legal purposes and to access only those systems, software, and data for which the user is authorized.

· College networks and electronic services are provided for uses consistent with the academic mission of the institution. They may not be used for commercial purposes nor for unsolicited advertising.

· Users are required to know and obey the specific policies established for the systems and networks they access. Under no circumstances may users give others access to College systems.

· College facilities may not be used to provide Wheaton network, Internet access, cable TV or telephone service to anyone outside of the Wheaton community for any purpose.

· The campus network is a shared resource. Therefore, network uses or applications which inhibit or interfere with the use of the network by others are not permitted (For example, applications which use an unusually high portion of network bandwidth for extended periods of time, thus inhibiting the use of the network by others, are not permitted).

· Information resources licensed by the College for the use of its students, faculty or staff may not be retransmitted outside of the College community. Examples include Project Muse, Encyclopedia Britannica (On-Line), site-licensed software, and commercial cable television service.

· Network, cable TV and telephone services and wiring may not be modified or extended beyond the area of their intended use. This applies to all wiring, hardware, and in-room jacks.

· Computer users may not assign an IP number to their machines. IP numbers are assigned dynamically. Manually assigning an IP number to one's machine may disrupt the network access of another user. Users with special needs may request a permanent IP number from the Director of IT&S.

Administrators of the network, computer systems and other electronic services have the responsibility to protect the rights of users, to set policies consistent with those rights, and to publicize those policies to their users. They have authority to control or refuse access to the network or other services to anyone who violates these policies or threatens the rights of other users.

Violations of the Acceptable Use Policy will be treated as violations of the Honor Code and will be referred to the Dean of Students Office for disciplinary action. Prosecution under State and Federal laws may also apply.

Contact: David Caldwell x3400
Last updated: 7/2000

Information Technology Services

Misuse of Information Technology Resource Privileges

The University characterizes misuse of computing and information resources and privileges as unethical and unacceptable and as just cause for taking disciplinary action. Misuse of computing and information resources and privileges includes, but is not restricted to, the following:

Attempting to modify or remove computer equipment, software, or peripherals without proper authorization.

Accessing computers, computer software, computer data or information, or networks without proper authorization, regardless of whether the computer, software, data, information, or network in question is owned by the University (That is, if you abuse the networks to which the University belongs or the computers at other sites connected to those networks, the University will treat this matter as an abuse of your William Paterson University computing privileges.)

Circumventing or attempting to circumvent normal resource limits, logon procedures, and security regulations, using computing facilities, computer accounts, or computer data for purposes other than those for which they were intended or authorized.

Unauthorized 'broadcast' distribution of email messages to users on or off campus sending fraudulent computer mail, breaking into another user's electronic mailbox, or reading someone else's electronic mail without his or her permission

Sending any fraudulent electronic transmission, including but not limited to fraudulent requests for confidential information.

Fraudulent submission of electronic purchase requisitions or journal vouchers, and fraudulent electronic authorization of purchase requisitions or journal vouchers violating any software license agreement or copyright, including copying or redistributing copyrighted computer software, data, or reports without proper, recorded authorization.

Violating the property rights of copyright holders who are in possession of computer-generated data, reports, or software

Using the University's computing resources to harass or threaten other users

Taking advantage of another user's naivete or negligence to gain access to any computer account, data, software, or file that is not your own and for which you have not received explicit authorization to access

Physically interfering with other users' access to the University's computing facilities encroaching on others' use of the University's computers (e.g., disrupting others' computer use by excessive game playing; by sending excessive messages, either locally or off-campus [including but not limited to electronic chain letters]; printing excessive copies of documents, files, data, or programs; modifying system facilities, operating systems, or disk partitions; attempting to crash or tie up a University computer; damaging or vandalizing University computing facilities, equipment, software, or computer files)

Disclosing or removing proprietary information, software, printed output or magnetic media without the explicit of the owner reading other users' data, information, files, or programs on a display screen, as printed output, or via electronic means, without the owner's explicit permission.

SELECTED URLS FOR POLICIES

SELECTED URLS FOR POLICIES

Library Policy URLS

LIBRARY POLICIES
ON COMPUTER USE

Adams State College
Nelsen Library
Alamosa, CO
>   http://www.library.adams.edu/student_computers.html

Arizona State University West
Fletcher Library
Phoenix, AZ
>   http://www.west.asu.edu/library/info/policy/internet_access_policy.html

Dakota State University
Karl E. Mundt Library
Madison, SD
>   http://www.departments.dsu.edu/personnel/policies/015100.htm

Francis Marion University
James A. Rogers Library
Florence, SC
>   http://vax.fmarion.edu/computer_use_pol.html

Lawrence University
Seeley G. Mudd Library
Appleton, WI
>   http://www.lawrence.edu/library/libinfo/aup.shtml

Otterbein College
Courtright Memorial Library
Westerville, OH
>   http://www.otterbein.edu/learning/libpages/compolic.htm

Seton Hill College
Reeves Memorial Library
Greensburg, PA
>   http://maura.setonhill.edu/~library/policies_computer.html

University of Southern Colorado
University Library
Pueblo, CO
>   http://library.uscolo.edu/compuse.html

Walla Walla College
Peterson Memorial Library
College Place, WA
http://www.wwc.edu/academics/library/cp/electronic_resources_policy

York College of PA
Schmidt Library
York, PA
http://www.ycp.edu/library/aup.html

SELECTED URLS FOR POLICIES

Institutional Policy URLS

INSTITUTIONAL POLICIES
ON COMPUTER USE

Alfred University
Herrick Library
Alfred, NY
       http://www.alfred.edu/its/policy.html

Arkansas Tech University
Pendergraft Library
Russellville, AR
       http://technology.atu.edu/cservices/computer-use.htm

Austin College
Abell Library Center
Sherman, TX
       http://abell.austinc.edu/Its/policies.html

Bentley College
Solmon R. Baker Library
Ultham, MA
       http://ecampus.bentley.edu/dept/aca/facmanual/APP_B002.htm

Bowdoin College
Bowdoin College Library
Brunswick, ME
       http://www.bowdoin.edu/dept/ccenter/policies/compuse.html

Christopher Newport University
Captain John Smith Library
Newport News, VA
       http://www.cnu.edu/cctr/policies1.html

Clarion University
Carlson Library
Clarion, PA
       http://www.clarion.edu/admin/compserv/common.htm

College of Saint Benedict/
St. John's University
Joint Libraries (Alcuin Library)
Collegeville, MN
       www.csbsju.edu/itservices/policies/termsandconditions.htm

Concordia College
Carl B. Yluisaker Library
Moorhead, NM
> http://www.cord.edu/dept/computing/policies/printing.html

Connecticut College
Charles E. Shain Library
New London, CT
> http://www.conncoll.edu/is/policy.html

Dakota State University
Karl E. Mundt Library
Madison, SD
> http://www.departments.dsu.edu/personnel/policies/036100.htm

Earlham College
Lilly Library
Richmond, IN
> http://www.earlham.edu/~ecs/html/policies/index.html

Emerson College
Boston, MA
> http://www.emerson.edu/policy/guidelines.html

Jacksonville State University
Houston Cole Library
Jacksonville, AL
> http://www.jsu.edu/depart/library/graphic/polcomp.htm

Mount Union College
Mount Union College Library
Alliance, OH
> http://www.muc.edu/cis/policies/Ethics.htm

Reed College
Eric Hauser Library
Portland, OR
> http://web.reed.edu/resources/cis/about/policies/acceptable.use.html

St. Olaf College
St. Olaf College Libraries
Northfield, MN
> http://www.stolaf.edu/services/iit/policies/misuse.html

SUNY Genesco
Milne Library
Genesco, NY
https://cit.geneseo.edu/policies/policies.html

Plattsburg State University of New York
Feinberg Library
Plattsburgh, NY
http://www2.plattsburgh.edu/acadvp/libinfo/compserv/policies/policy10.html
http://www2.plattsburgh.edu/acadvp/libinfo/compserv/policies/

Tarleton State University
Dick Smith Library
Stephenville, TX
http://www.tarleton.edu/~tiic/networkpolicy.htm

University of Richmond
University of Richmond Libraries
University of Richmond, VA
http://www.richmond.edu/is/info/Technology-policies.html

University of Southern Colorado
University Library
Pueblo, CO
http://www.uscolo.edu/info/ecommpolicy.html

Upper Iowa University
Henderson-Wilder Library
Lafette, IA
http://www.uiu.edu/Prospective_Students/Residential/resources/Computer/computer_usage.html

Wartburg College
Vogel Library
Waverly, IA
http://www.wartburg.edu/compserv/policy.html

Wellesley College
Wellesley College Library
Wellesley, MA
http://www.wellesley.edu/acceptuse.html

West Virginia State College
Drain-Jordan Library
Institute, WV
http://www.wvsc.edu/admin/use_and_abuse.html

Wheaton College
Madeleine Clark Wallace Library
Norton, MA
http://www.wheatoncollege.edu/it&s/policies/aup.ssi

William Paterson University
Askew Library
Wayne, NJ
http://www.wpunj.edu/itservices/policies/wpu_mitr.htm